Cynthia L. Greene

SOUTH-WESTERN
THOMSON LEARNING

Australia • Canada • Mexico • Singapore • Spain • United Kingdom • United States

COPYRIGHT

Business 2000
Selling
by Cynthia L. Greene

Vice President/Executive Publisher
Dave Shaut

Team Leader
Karen Schmohe

Executive Editor
Eve Lewis

Project Manager
Enid Nagel

Production Manager
Patricia Matthews Boies

Editor
Colleen A. Farmer

Executive Marketing Manager
Carol Volz

Channel Manager
Nancy A. Long

Marketing Coordinator
Yvonne Patton-Beard

Manufacturing Coordinator
Kevin L. Kluck

Art and Design Coordinator
Tippy McIntosh

Cover and Internal Design
Bill Spencer

Editorial Assistant
Stephanie L. White

Production Assistant
Nancy Stamper

Compositor
New England Typographic Service

Printer
Courier, Kendallville

About the Author
Cynthia L. Greene taught business education at the high school level for 25 years. She taught in the Fulton County School System at Centennial High School in Roswell, Georgia, where she was a Cooperative Business Education Coordinator and chair of the business and career technology department. She has been active in the National Business Education Association, serving on the Entrepreneurship Standards Committee and as a writer for the Entrepreneurship Lesson Plans. She recently served as president of the Southern Business Education Association.

Copyright © 2003 South-Western, a division of Thomson Learning, Inc. Thomson Learning™ is a trademark used herein under license.

ISBN: 0-538-43145-8

Printed in the United States of America
1 2 3 4 5 6 CK 05 04 03 02 01

ALL RIGHTS RESERVED. No part of this work covered by copyright hereon may be reproduced or used in any form or by any means—graphic, electronic, or mechanical, including photocopying, recording, taping, Web distribution or information storage and retrieval systems—without the written permission of the publisher.

For permission to use material from this text or product, contact us by

Tel: 800-730-2214
Fax: 800-730-2215
Web: www.thomsonrights.com

For more information, contact South-Western, 5191 Natorp Boulevard, Mason, OH, 45040. Or you can visit our Internet site at

www.swep.com

International Divisions List

Asia (including India)
Thomson Learning
60 Albert Street, #15-01
Albert Complex
Singapore 189969
Tel 65 336-6411
Fax 65 336-7411

Australia/New Zealand
Nelson
102 Dobbs Street
South Melbourne
Victoria 3205
Australia
Tel 61 (0)3 9685-4111
Fax 61 (0)3 9685-4199

Canada
Nelson
1120 Birchmount Road
Toronto, Ontario
Canada M1K 5G4
Tel (416) 752-9100
Fax (416) 752-8102

Latin America
Thomson Learning
Seneca 53
Colonia Polanco
11560 Mexico, D.F. Mexico
Tel (525) 281-2906
Fax (525) 281-2656

Spain (including Portugal)
Paraninfo
Calle Magallanes 25
28015 Madrid
Espana
Tel 34 (0)91 446-3350
Fax 34 (0)91 445-6218

UK/Europe/Middle East/Africa
Thomson Learning
Berkshire House
168-173 High Holborn
London WC 1V 7AA
United Kingdom
Tel 44 (0)20 497-1422
Fax 44 (0)20 497-1426

YOUR COURSE PLANNING JUST GOT EASIER!

NEW! Business 2000 is an exciting new modular instructional program that allows you to create customized courses or enhance already existing curriculum.

Selling by Cynthia L. Greene
0-538-43145-8   Learner Guide

Marketing by James L. Burrow
0-538-43133-4   Learner Guide

E-Commerce by Dotty Boen Oelkers
0-538-69880-2   Learner Guide

Advertising by Maria Townsley
0-538-69870-5   Learner Guide

Entrepreneurship by Cynthia L. Greene
0-538-69875-6   Learner Guide

Retail by Maria Townsley
0-538-43156-3   Learner Guide

Customer Service by Career Solutions Training Group
0-538-43126-1   Learner Guide

International Business by Les R. Dlabay
0-538-43139-3   Learner Guide

Multimedia Module and Instructor Support Materials Also Available

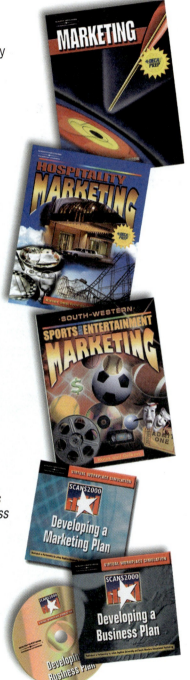

NEW! *Marketing* by Burrow
A new program that integrates the full range of DECA competencies and the National Marketing Education foundations and functions of marketing.

0-538-43232-2   Student Text

NEW! *Hospitality Marketing* by Kaser and Freeman
Covers the marketing curriculum using the hospitality industry as the learning vehicle.

0-538-43208-X   Student Text

Sports and Entertainment Marketing by Kaser and Oelkers
Takes you on a step-by-step journey through the world of marketing in the exciting world of sports and entertainment.

0-538-69477-7   Student Text

SCANS 2000 Virtual Workplace Simulations in partnership with Johns Hopkins University
These CD-based simulations create a challenging, interactive workplace experience. Learners develop and apply their academic and soft skills in a real-world setting while creating business and marketing plans.

0-538-69827-6   Developing a Business Plan
0-538-69819-5   Developing a Marketing Plan

Join Us on the Internet   www.swep.com

HOW TO USE THIS BOOK
ENGAGE STUDENT INTEREST

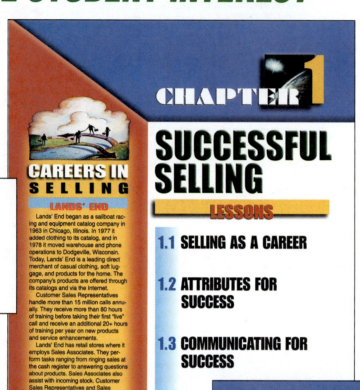

CAREERS IN SELLING
Highlights a real-world company and how it uses selling.

LESSONS
Make the text easy to use in all classroom environments.

VIDEO
Contains clips from several resources that can be used to introduce concepts in each chapter.

PROJECT
Group or individual activity that has activities for each lesson.

HOW TO USE THIS BOOK

CHAPTER 1 SUCCESSFUL SELLING

LESSON 1.1
SELLING AS A CAREER

EXPLAIN the concept of selling

EXPLORE career opportunities in sales

GOALS
Begin each lesson and offer an overview.

THE ART OF SELLING

You may have heard someone referred to as a "born salesperson." Even though this term is often used to describe a very successful salesperson, no one is a born salesperson. Selling is a learned art. You may possess some of the attributes of a good salesperson but it takes training and practice to become successful. A successful salesperson has product knowledge, sales experience, and the ability to persuade.

SELLING IS ALL AROUND YOU

Selling does not just take place in stores. Businesspeople must sell coworkers on ideas when they want to make changes in a business. Children "sell" to their parents daily as they try to convince them that what they want is a good idea. Any time one person tries to persuade another to do something or act a certain way, a form of selling is taking place.

Many people described Richard Ramey as a "born salesperson." While in school, he was always the top salesperson in every school fundraiser. What characteristics do you think Richard possessed that made him so successful in sales?

ON THE SCENE
Lesson opening scenario that provides motivation.

1.1 SELLING AS A CAREER

meet their needs. Customers will not purchase a product or service until they are convinced that they will benefit from owning that product or service.

WHAT DOES A SALESPERSON DO?

People often have trouble deciding on a product and need the assistance of a salesperson to make a final decision. A salesperson explains, advises, and assists the customer in making a wise buying decision. The objective of any sale is to have a satisfied customer because a satisfied customer will become a repeat customer. A **repeat customer** is one who returns to shop at a certain business.

A CAREER IN SALES

Between 1998 and 2008, two sales occupations are projected by the Bureau of Labor Statistics to be among the top ten occupations with the largest growth. These occupations are retail salesperson, with a 14 percent projected increase, and cashier, with a 17 percent projected increase. Career opportunities exist not only in retail sales but also in other areas, such as insurance, securities, real estate, financial services, and manufacturing. According to data from the Bureau of Labor Statistics, job opportunities for securities, commodities, and financial service sales agents are predicted to increase 41 percent from 1998 to 2008. There is a projected need for 427,000 employees in this area by 2008.

Selling also plays an important role in many other careers not classified as sales careers. Some of these positions include entrepreneurs, managers, accountants, contractors, information technology specialists, and attorneys.

In a group, brainstorm to produce a list of businesses and the products or services they sell.

WORKSHOP
Provides activities to use in class.

Why is selling important to a business?

CHECKPOINT
Short questions within lessons to assist with reading and to assure students are grasping concepts.

SPECIAL FEATURES ENHANCE LEARNING

Write a sales letter to a friend about one of your favorite products. Remember the object of the letter is to get the reader's attention.

COMMUNICATE Provides activities to reinforce, review, and practice communication skills.

BUSINESS ETIQUETTE

When using a personal selling approach with people from other countries, you should take time to learn the business etiquette followed in that country. Using an inappropriate gesture, greeting, word, or business procedure may result in lost sales. Something accepted as a common practice in the United States may be considered rude and offensive in another country. For example, Americans move quickly to the business aspect of a sales call. However, in Latin America and the Far East, all meetings begin with a period of social conversation.

THINK CRITICALLY What are some things you can do when preparing to do business with people from other countries?

WORLD VIEW Provides international business connections relevant to today's current events.

E-COMMERCE Electronic commerce is growing rapidly. Many people wonder what long-term effect e-commerce will have on traditional retailing. Many companies now have web sites. Some of these web sites offer products for sale to consumers while others offer products for sale to other businesses. Some businesses use their Internet site to provide information about their company and products. The Internet makes it easy for shoppers to see new product lines without having to travel to a store or a showroom. However, as Internet shopping grows, the need for retail salespeople will decline.

THINK CRITICALLY Why do you think someone would choose to shop on the Internet instead of going to a traditional retail store?

TECH TALK Provides information about new technology that is being used in business.

Consumer spending is declining in the retail market. Just below one-third, 32.9%, of all consumer spending took place in the retail sector in 2000. This compares with 47% in 1980.

DID YOU KNOW? Provides an interesting fact about the topic.

Dedicated web site b2000.swep.com that provides activities and links for each chapter.

BUSINESS MATH CONNECTION

Many sales representatives are paid on commission. A commission is a percentage of sales. If Ruiz Perez earns a 7 percent commission on every home he sells, what would his commission be if he sold one home for $110,000, one home for $145,000, and one home for $210,000?

SOLUTION
Add the total amount of sales. Then multiply the total by the percentage amount of Ruiz's commission. Ruiz's commission would be $32,550.

$110,000 + $145,000 + $210,000 = $465,000
$465,000 × 0.07 = $32,550

BUSINESS MATH CONNECTION Worked example that reinforces and reviews math concepts.

ASSESSMENT AND REVIEW

HOW TO USE THIS BOOK

END-OF-LESSON ACTIVITIES

Think Critically Provides opportunities to apply concepts.
Make Connections Provides connections to other disciplines.

Presentation Icon indicates opportunity to use presentation software, such as PowerPoint.

Word Processing Icon indicates opportunity to use word processing software.

Spreadsheet Icon indicates opportunity to use spreadsheet software.

Internet Icon indicates opportunity to research on the web.

CHAPTER REVIEW Contains Chapter Summary, Vocabulary Builder, Review Concepts, Apply What You Learned, Make Connections

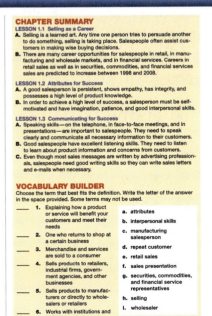

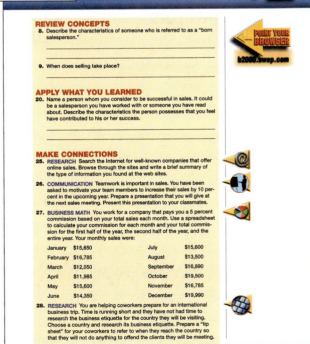

CONTENTS

SUCCESSFUL SELLING 2

CAREERS IN SELLING
Lands' End 2

PROJECT
Is a Career in Sales for You? 3

Lesson 1.1 Selling as a Career 4
Lesson 1.2 Attributes for Success 9
Lesson 1.3 Communicating for Success 14

ASSESSMENT AND REVIEW
Checkpoint 5, 7, 10, 12, 16, 17, 18
Think Critically 8, 13, 19
Make Connections 8, 13, 19
Chapter Review 20–23

SPECIAL FEATURES
Business Math Connection 6
Communicate 17
Did You Know? 6
On the Scene 4, 9, 14
Tech Talk 6
Workshop 5, 10, 17
World View 11

TECHNOLOGY AND SELLING 24

CAREERS IN SELLING
Charles Schwab & Co., Inc. 24

PROJECT
Technology and Selling 25

Lesson 2.1 Telemarketing and Customer Data 26
Lesson 2.2 The Internet and Multimedia 31
Lesson 2.3 Use Technology for Follow-Up 37

ASSESSMENT AND REVIEW
Checkpoint 28, 29, 33, 35, 39, 40
Think Critically 30, 36, 41
Make Connections 30, 36, 41
Chapter Review 42–45

SPECIAL FEATURES
Business Math Connection 38
Communicate 39
Did You Know? 27
On the Scene 26, 31, 37
Tech Talk 29
Workshop 29, 34, 39
World View 32

CHAPTER 3

PREPARING TO SELL 46

CAREERS IN SELLING
Borders, Inc. 46

PROJECT
Preparing to Sell 47

Lesson 3.1 Psychology of Selling 48
Lesson 3.2 Knowledge for Selling 54
Lesson 3.3 Prospecting for Sales 59

ASSESSMENT AND REVIEW
Checkpoint 50, 52, 56, 57, 62, 64
Think Critically 53, 58, 65
Make Connections 53, 58, 65
Chapter Review 66–69

SPECIAL FEATURES
Business Math Connection 57
Communicate 52
Did You Know? 51
On the Scene 48, 54, 59
Tech Talk 62
Workshop 49, 56, 61
World View 55

CHAPTER 4

DEVELOPING THE SALE 70

CAREERS IN SELLING
Creative Memories 70

PROJECT
Planning the Sale 71

Lesson 4.1 The Pre-Approach 72
Lesson 4.2 Meeting a Need 78
Lesson 4.3 Handling Objections 85

ASSESSMENT AND REVIEW
Checkpoint 73, 75, 76, 80, 83, 87, 89, 90
Think Critically 77, 84, 91
Make Connections 77, 84, 91
Chapter Review 92–95

SPECIAL FEATURES
Business Math Connection 82
Communicate 74
Did You Know? 73
On the Scene 72, 78, 85
Tech Talk 74
Workshop 75, 81, 89
World View 89

CONTENTS

CLOSING AND BEYOND 96

CAREERS IN SELLING
Delta Airlines 96

PROJECT
Closing the Sale 97

Lesson 5.1 Closing and the Sales Process 98
Lesson 5.2 Methods of Closing 107
Lesson 5.3 After the Sale 114

ASSESSMENT AND REVIEW
Checkpoint 101, 105, 108, 111, 112, 117, 119, 120
Think Critically 106, 113, 121
Make Connections 106, 113, 121
Chapter Review 122–125

SPECIAL FEATURES
Business Math Connection 118
Communicate 105
Did You Know? 109
On the Scene 98, 107, 114
Tech Talk 108
Workshop 101, 110, 119
World View 116

RETAIL SELLING 126

CAREERS IN SELLING
The Home Depot 126

PROJECT
Retail Selling Process 127

Lesson 6.1 Basics of Retail Selling 128
Lesson 6.2 Sales Process in Retail Selling 137
Lesson 6.3 Other Skills for Retail Selling 146

ASSESSMENT AND REVIEW
Checkpoint 131, 135, 140, 143, 144, 147, 150, 152
Think Critically 136, 145, 153
Make Connections 136, 145, 153
Chapter Review 154–157

SPECIAL FEATURES
Business Math Connection 151
Communicate 147
Did You Know? 130
On the Scene 128, 137, 146
Tech Talk 130
Workshop 129, 139, 152
World View 143

Glossary 158
Index 161
Photo Credits 166

REVIEWERS

Patricia J. Adolfs
Auburn Hills, MI

Carol Ann Allen
Warwick, RI

Edward B. Bufford
Phoenix, AZ

Cheryl Fulton
Burke, VA

Tracie Holub
Rosenberg, TX

Sissy Long
Pensacola, FL

Vicki McKay
Pasadena, TX

Debbi Popo
Columbus, OH

Edward Pregitzer
Cincinnati, OH

Anne Jansen Wardinski
Burke, VA

CHAPTER 1

SUCCESSFUL SELLING

LESSONS

1.1 SELLING AS A CAREER

1.2 ATTRIBUTES FOR SUCCESS

1.3 COMMUNICATING FOR SUCCESS

CAREERS IN SELLING

LANDS' END

Lands' End began as a sailboat racing and equipment catalog company in 1963 in Chicago, Illinois. In 1977 it added clothing to its catalog, and in 1978 it moved warehouse and phone operations to Dodgeville, Wisconsin. Today, Lands' End is a leading direct merchant of casual clothing, soft luggage, and products for the home. The company's products are offered through its catalogs and via the Internet.

Customer Sales Representatives handle more than 15 million calls annually. They receive more than 80 hours of training before taking their first "live" call and receive an additional 20+ hours of training per year on new products and service enhancements.

Lands' End has retail stores where it employs Sales Associates. They perform tasks ranging from ringing sales at the cash register to answering questions about products. Sales Associates also assist with incoming stock. Customer Sales Representatives and Sales Associates should have excellent communication skills and the ability to interpret a situation and act appropriately.

THINK CRITICALLY

1. What strategies has Lands' End used to remain a leader in catalog sales?
2. Would you prefer a position as a Customer Sales Representative or a Sales Associate? Why?

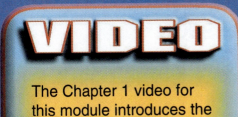

The Chapter 1 video for this module introduces the concepts in this chapter.

Is a Career in Sales For You?

PROJECT OBJECTIVES
- Explore careers in sales
- Examine your attributes to determine if you could be successful in a sales career
- Develop communication skills for success

GETTING STARTED
Read through the Project Process below. Make a list of any materials you will need. Decide how you will get the needed materials or information.
- Look for information about careers in sales. Find out about the types of tasks that are performed in these jobs. Does a career in sales interest you?
- Find out what types of skills salespersons use on the job. Do you have these skills?
- Evaluate your oral and written communication skills. Do you need to improve any of these skills?

PROJECT PROCESS

Part 1 **LESSON 1.1** Using the Internet and information from the Chamber of Commerce, media center, and other resources, research careers in sales. Determine which are projected to have increased demand in your area. Choose one of these careers and learn more about it.

Part 2 **LESSON 1.2** Make a list of the attributes and communication skills that are needed for success in the career you have selected. Design a chart listing the attributes and communication skills. Use a rating scale from 1 to 5, with 1 representing "Do Not Possess" and 5 representing "I'm the Best!" Rate yourself on each of the skills using your rating chart.

Part 3 **LESSON 1.3** Determine which attributes and communication skills you need to improve in order to be successful in the sales career you have chosen. Develop a plan for improvement.

CHAPTER REVIEW

Project Wrap-up Prepare a presentation on the attributes and communication skills that are necessary for success in the sales career you selected and present it to your classmates.

CHAPTER 1 SUCCESSFUL SELLING

LESSON 1.1
SELLING AS A CAREER

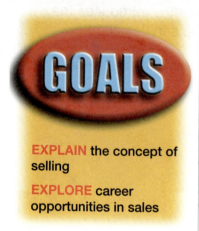

EXPLAIN the concept of selling

EXPLORE career opportunities in sales

THE ART OF SELLING

You may have heard someone referred to as a "born salesperson." Even though this term is often used to describe a very successful salesperson, no one is a born salesperson. Selling is a learned art. You may possess some of the attributes of a good salesperson but it takes training and practice to become successful. A successful salesperson has product knowledge, sales experience, and the ability to persuade.

SELLING IS ALL AROUND YOU

Selling does not just take place in stores. Businesspeople must sell coworkers on ideas when they want to make changes in a business. Children "sell" to their parents daily as they try to convince them that what they want is a good idea. Any time one person tries to persuade another to do something or act a certain way, a form of selling is taking place.

ON THE $CENE

Many people described Richard Ramey as a "born salesperson." While in school, he was always the top salesperson in every school fundraiser. What characteristics do you think Richard possessed that made him so successful in sales?

1.1 SELLING AS A CAREER

WHAT IS SELLING?
Selling involves the art of communicating effectively with people. It is the process of explaining how a product or service will benefit your customers and meet their needs. Customers will not purchase a product or service until they are convinced that they will benefit from owning that product or service.

WHAT DOES A SALESPERSON DO?
People often have trouble deciding on a product and need the assistance of a salesperson to make a final decision. A salesperson explains, advises, and assists the customer in making a wise buying decision. The objective of any sale is to have a satisfied customer because a satisfied customer will become a repeat customer. A **repeat customer** is one who returns to shop at a certain business.

In a group, brainstorm to produce a list of businesses and the products or services they sell.

A CAREER IN SALES
Between 1998 and 2008, two sales occupations are projected by the Bureau of Labor Statistics to be among the top ten occupations with the largest growth. These occupations are retail salesperson, with a 14 percent projected increase, and cashier, with a 17 percent projected increase. Career opportunities exist not only in retail sales but also in other areas, such as insurance, securities, real estate, financial services, and manufacturing. According to data from the Bureau of Labor Statistics, job opportunities for securities, commodities, and financial service sales agents are predicted to increase 41 percent from 1998 to 2008. There is a projected need for 427,000 employees in this area by 2008.

Selling also plays an important role in many other careers not classified as sales careers. Some of these positions include entrepreneurs, managers, accountants, contractors, information technology specialists, and attorneys.

CHECKPOINT
Why is selling important to a business?

CHAPTER 1 SUCCESSFUL SELLING

BUSINESS MATH CONNECTION

Many sales representatives are paid on commission. A commission is a percentage of sales. If Ruiz Perez earns a 7 percent commission on every home he sells, what would his commission be if he sold one home for $110,000, one home for $145,000, and one home for $210,000?

SOLUTION
Add the total amount of sales. Then multiply the total by the percentage amount of Ruiz's commission. Ruiz's commission would be $32,550.

$110,000 + $145,000 + $210,000 = $465,000
$465,000 × 0.07 = $32,550

did you KNOW?

Consumer spending is declining in the retail market. Just below one-third, 32.9%, of all consumer spending took place in the retail sector in 2000. This compares with 47% in 1980.

CAREER OPPORTUNITIES IN SALES

Selling occurs in many different places and at many different levels. You are probably most familiar with **retail sales** where a salesperson sells merchandise and services to a consumer. A **wholesaler** sells products to retailers, other wholesalers, industrial firms, government agencies, or other businesses. A **manufacturing salesperson** sells products to other manufacturers or directly to wholesalers or retailers. **Securities, commodities, and financial service representatives** work with institutions and individuals who want to invest money. These sales representatives buy and sell stocks, bonds, shares in mutual funds, insurance commodities, and other financial products.

RETAIL SALES

Retail sales take place in retail stores. You have probably shopped in many retail stores. These stores include department stores, supermarkets, drug stores,

E-COMMERCE Electronic commerce is growing rapidly. Many people wonder what long-term effect e-commerce will have on traditional retailing. Many companies now have web sites. Some of these web sites offer products for sale to consumers while others offer products for sale to other businesses. Some businesses use their Internet site to provide information about their company and products. The Internet makes it easy for shoppers to see new product lines without having to travel to a store or a showroom. However, as Internet shopping grows, the need for retail salespeople will decline.

THINK CRITICALLY Why do you think someone would choose to shop on the Internet instead of going to a traditional retail store?

1.1 SELLING AS A CAREER

discount stores, jewelry stores, and convenience stores. Restaurants, hair salons, and nail salons also are considered to be retail stores. In retail stores, merchandise and services are sold to the final consumer or end user of the merchandise and services. Different retail stores take different approaches to selling.

Personal Selling In some retail stores, the personal selling approach is important to customers. These stores hire their sales staff to sell products and services personally to consumers. Department stores, jewelry stores, and automobile dealerships depend on their sales staff to use a personal selling approach. In the personal selling approach, the sales staff is responsible for approaching customers, explaining the features and benefits of products, demonstrating products, answering customers' questions, and closing sales.

Self-Service Some retail stores hire cashiers or clerks. Discount stores, convenience stores, supermarkets, and many gas stations fall into this category. In self-service stores, customers choose their merchandise with little or no assistance and pay a cashier or clerk for their selections.

MANUFACTURERS AND WHOLESALE SALES REPRESENTATIVES

These sales representatives serve as intermediaries and sell merchandise to retailers, manufacturers, and other wholesalers. The primary duties of manufacturers and wholesale sales representatives are to interest wholesale and retail buyers and purchasing agents in their merchandise and to address the questions or concerns of the clients. They also offer advice to clients on ways to use their products, reduce costs, and increase sales.

FINANCIAL SALES

As more individuals are looking to invest money, there is a projected employment increase for securities, commodities, and financial services sales representatives. The clients of these sales representatives range from individuals with small amounts of money to large institutions with millions of dollars to invest.

Securities and Commodities Sales Representatives These representatives, also called brokers, stockbrokers, account executives, or financial consultants, perform a variety of duties. These duties include bringing together buyers and sellers of securities and commodities, managing investments, and offering financial advice.

Financial Services Sales Representatives Selling, banking, and related services are the primary duties of these sales representatives. Some of the services they sell include deposit accounts, lines of credit, certificates of deposit, cash management, and investment services. This category includes financial planners who provide financial plans tailored to their clients' needs. They use their knowledge of tax and investment strategies, securities, insurance, pension plans, and real estate in developing these plans.

Describe three different types of sales.

7

THINK CRITICALLY

1. Describe the traits of a successful salesperson.

2. Give an example of selling that does not involve the exchange of a good or service for money.

3. Describe a positive and a negative retail sales transaction in which you recently participated.

4. Describe the following types of selling approaches: retail with personal selling approach and retail with self-service approach.

MAKE CONNECTIONS

5. **RESEARCH** Use the library or Internet to research the job responsibilities of a career in sales that is of interest to you. Also, find out what training and experience is required for the career. Present your findings to the class.

6. **COMMUNICATION** Interview someone who works in a sales occupation. Find what the person does, the hours the person works, the education and training required for the position, and ways the job has changed in the last two years. Prepare a one-page report on your findings.

7. **COMMUNICATION** Working with a group, brainstorm to develop a list of benefits that would sell your school principal on the idea that your school's prom should be held in outer space.

8. **BUSINESS MATH** You have interviewed for a sales position at two stores. Company A has offered to pay you $100 plus 5 percent of your total monthly sales. The average monthly sales per employee is $27,500. Company B has offered to pay you $1,300 per month. Which job would you choose?

LESSON 1.2
ATTRIBUTES FOR SUCCESS

1.2 ATTRIBUTES FOR SUCCESS

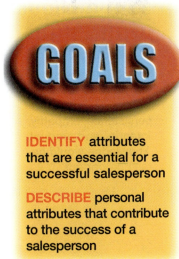

IDENTIFY attributes that are essential for a successful salesperson

DESCRIBE personal attributes that contribute to the success of a salesperson

ESSENTIAL ATTRIBUTES

There are many **attributes**, or personality characteristics, that contribute to the success of a salesperson. Personal attributes include self-motivation, imagination, patience, and interpersonal skills. However, the basic attributes of persistence, empathy, integrity, and knowledge of the product are essential to a salesperson's success.

PERSISTENCE

Persistence is being unwilling to take no for an answer. Many times, a salesperson is not received with a warm welcome. After several disappointing encounters, a salesperson who lacks persistence might decide to give up.

ON THE $CENE

Before Richard started selling items for school fundraisers, he studied the products being sold and learned all that he could about them. If the product was one that would appeal to his classmates, he talked to some of them to see what they thought about it. If the product appealed to adults, he talked to his parents and teachers. Once he started selling, he didn't take "no" for an answer. He could always devise a reason for his customers to purchase the item he was selling. What do you think Richard did that contributed to his success in selling the products?

CHAPTER 1 SUCCESSFUL SELLING

In a group, brainstorm to produce a list of situations in which persistence, empathy, integrity, and product knowledge would be important.

Salespersons deal with many different types of individuals and face new situations daily. A good salesperson will not be discouraged by these situations and will continue to try until the sale is made or all options are exhausted.

EMPATHY

Empathy is the ability to understand the situation from the other person's perspective. You may not have been in a situation similar to that person, but you can put yourself in the customer's place and understand how he feels. This helps a salesperson know what to say and what to do in order to encourage a customer to make a purchase.

INTEGRITY

Integrity is the ability to distinguish between right and wrong and to make decisions based on that distinction. Integrity involves more than just following the law. It involves following behaviors that are generally acknowledged by members of society as acceptable. Your ethics are those values and beliefs that are based on your integrity. Many people who are considered unethical have not broken the law, but they have not followed acceptable social practices.

KNOWLEDGE OF THE PRODUCT

When customers are making a purchase, they often look to the salesperson to educate them about the product or service. If salespeople are not knowledgeable about the product or service they are selling, they will lose credibility with their customers, and this will result in a loss of sales. Salespeople also must be knowledgeable about products of competitors in order to persuade customers to purchase their products.

CHECKPOINT

Why are persistence, empathy, integrity, and knowledge of the product important attributes for a salesperson?

1.2 ATTRIBUTES FOR SUCCESS

DM FLS WORLD VIEW

BUSINESS ETIQUETTE

When using a personal selling approach with people from other countries, you should take time to learn the business etiquette followed in that country. Using an inappropriate gesture, greeting, word, or business procedure may result in lost sales. Something accepted as a common practice in the United States may be considered rude and offensive in another country. For example, Americans move quickly to the business aspect of a sales call. However, in Latin America and the Far East, all meetings begin with a period of social conversation.

THINK CRITICALLY What are some things you can do when preparing to do business with people from other countries?

PERSONAL ATTRIBUTES

As you move into more sophisticated selling situations, certain personal attributes become more important. These include self-motivation, imagination, patience, and interpersonal skills.

SELF-MOTIVATION

Self-motivation is the ability to control your own activities. Retail sales positions usually are closely supervised by a manager and do not require the same amount of self-motivation that someone working in the field would need. Salespeople in the field usually set their own appointments and work with potential clients to find the product or service that best meets their needs. It is important for these individuals to be able to recognize what needs to be done and then to act on it with little or no supervision.

IMAGINATION

Imagination is the ability to apply creativity to a specific situation. Creative thinking is important for many salespeople. A creative salesperson must be able to help customers see the benefits the product or service will provide to them, oftentimes without the product or service actually being there.

Imagination is often important in developing a new sales technique. You may come across a sales situation where a technique that had been successful in past experiences is no longer effective. It will be important for you to use your imagination and create a new technique to try.

PATIENCE

Patience is the ability to keep your emotions out of the sales process in order to make the sale and benefit the client. You may spend quite a bit of time working with a client and be eager to finalize a sale, but the client may need more time. It is important for you to remain patient with the client. Salespersons who show impatience or pressure a client for a decision often lose sales.

You may hear the same objections from many different clients. Remember to remain patient because even though you have heard the objection before, this is the first time this particular client has used the objection.

INTERPERSONAL SKILLS

Interpersonal skills are those skills that help you work well with others. As a salesperson you will always be working with others, and it is important for you to get along with your customers or clients. You should always show an interest in the ideas and concerns of clients and customers. Showing interest in their needs will help to build their confidence in you.

Teamwork Although many salespeople work individually with customers, they are usually part of a team. When working as a team, all members should be focused on the same objectives. If a team has been given the goal of increasing sales by 10 percent, it will be important for members to work together to determine their strategy for reaching the goal and then for all members to do their part to achieve the goal.

Team Leader You may become the leader of the sales team during your career. As the team leader, it will be your responsibility to lead your sales team to become an outstanding team. Team members will take their lead from you. If you are enthusiastic and positive about what you are doing, your team members will share your positive attitude. Always be on the lookout for outstanding salespeople. You never know when you may have to fill an opening on your team, and it is better to have a prospect list ready than to have to search for a replacement in a short amount of time. A good sales team leader will make calls with the members of the team. You will have a better idea about what is going on if you are out in the field observing what your salespeople are experiencing. This will also help you see the strengths and weaknesses of the team members and enable you to work with them in a positive manner.

CHECKPOINT

What are the personal attributes of a successful salesperson?
___
___

1.2 ATTRIBUTES FOR SUCCESS

THINK CRITICALLY

1. Give an example of a situation where you showed persistence. Why was it important for you to be persistent?
   _____
   _____
   _____

2. Why is product knowledge important for a salesperson? Could it have an effect on a customer's decision to purchase a product or service?
   _____
   _____
   _____
   _____

3. Describe the characteristics of an individual who is self-motivated.
   _____
   _____
   _____
   _____

4. Explain why patience is an important attribute of a salesperson, and describe a situation you have experienced where a salesperson showed a great deal of patience.
   _____
   _____
   _____
   _____

MAKE CONNECTIONS

5. **PROBLEM SOLVING** With a partner, role play an example of how to get along with a difficult person in a sales situation.

6. **PROBLEM SOLVING** You are working as a member of a team that is trying to capture 25 percent of the market for a new product your company is introducing. There is one member of the team who is not making assigned calls or looking for new customer leads. The other team members are becoming frustrated with this individual. Develop a strategy to work with this team member to encourage him to do his fair share in reaching the goal.

7. **COMMUNICATION** Using the Internet, research business etiquette of another country. With a partner, role play a business meeting with someone from that country by applying what you have learned.

8. **COMMUNICATION** You are going to visit another school to recruit salespeople for a new store opening in your area. Prepare a multimedia presentation to help the students understand the attributes you are looking for in applicants that will help ensure their success in sales.

LESSON 1.3
COMMUNICATING FOR SUCCESS

GOALS

DEVELOP speaking skills for success

DEVELOP effective listening skills

EXPLAIN the purpose of written sales material

SUCCESSFUL SPEAKING

A career in sales requires excellent communication skills. Throughout the steps of a sale, you will be involved in face-to-face and/or telephone communication with potential customers, and your communication ability will play an important role in their decision to buy.

TELEPHONE CONVERSATIONS

You may make an initial contact with potential customers by telephone, or you may call to give them information or to set up a meeting. You should follow these tips for effective telephone conversations.

1. *Speak clearly and talk directly into the receiver.* Remove gum or candy from your mouth before making the call or answering the telephone.

ON THE $CENE

Richard knew that communication skills were important if he was going to make a good impression on customers. He knew he had to speak clearly and listen to people when he was trying to make a sale. Before he attempted to sell a product for a school fundraiser, he practiced what he was going to say to be sure that he described all of the product's features. Why do you think Richard spent time preparing before starting to sell?

1.3 COMMUNICATING FOR SUCCESS

2. ***Speak politely.*** Do not use improper language. Be respectful, and do not interrupt.

3. ***Outline the material you want to cover.*** Before making a call, you should write down the points you want to make and any technical information you plan to share. This will ensure that you cover everything you intended to and that you do not give incorrect information.

4. ***Take notes.*** This will help you remember all of the important details.

MEETINGS

Much of the sales process takes place during face-to-face meetings with potential customers. Whenever you have a planned meeting with a potential customer, you should spend time preparing for the meeting so you will make a good impression. Follow these tips to help your meetings run smoothly.

1. ***Shake hands and make eye contact with the person you are meeting.*** Introduce yourself if this is your first meeting. Use the customer's name if you know it. If the customer introduces herself to you, immediately use her name. This will help you remember it.

2. ***Speak clearly.*** Speak at a volume that is not too loud or too soft and enunciate your words.

3. ***When the customer speaks, show an interest in what he is saying.*** Provide responses to the customer's questions and ask questions to gather more information from him.

4. ***Do not be rushed or anxious to be somewhere else.*** Schedule meetings for times that are convenient so that you can devote your full attention to the customer.

5. ***Thank the customer at the end of the meeting.*** Let the customer know when you will contact her again and how to contact you if she needs more information.

PRESENTATION

A **sales presentation** is the part of the sales process when the salesperson explains how a product or service will benefit the customer. Product knowledge is important for an effective presentation. In addition to having product knowledge, a good salesperson will learn all available information about the audience before the presentation. An effective sales presentation will inform the potential customer about product benefits not previously known and then will persuade the listener to take action. When presenting sales information to the audience, the salesperson may want to use a multimedia program that is operated from a computer or may decide to use printed materials.

The next step in preparing a presentation is to put all information in a logical sequence. The presenter should then practice the presentation several times to be sure everything is in order before presenting the information to the audience. An outline would be helpful to use when presenting the material.

CHECKPOINT

What are some tips for successful speaking?

_____
_____

EFFECTIVE LISTENING

More than 50 percent of a typical day is spent listening. Although hearing and listening are related, they are different processes. Hearing is simply a physical process, but listening combines hearing with understanding. To be

successful in sales, it is important for you to listen carefully. You will listen to presentations on new products and services you will be selling. You will need to be attentive during these presentations because you will have to communicate this information to clients.

You will need to listen carefully to customers as they express their ideas or concerns about the product you are selling. Information you gather from listening to customers will help you as you move through the sales process.

Many times you may try to listen to someone talk, but a *barrier* may interfere with your listening. A barrier may be a noise or a distraction, but it also may come from feelings such as boredom or stress. As a salesperson, you must work to overcome these barriers and not let them affect the listening process when you are listening to others.

1.3 COMMUNICATING FOR SUCCESS

TIPS FOR EFFECTIVE LISTENING
The following tips will help you become a more effective listener.

1. *Focus your attention on the person who is speaking.* Do not let any barriers distract you. Clear your mind and give the person who is speaking your undivided attention.
2. *Think about and try to understand what the other person is saying.*
3. *Ask questions to make sure you understand what the person is saying.* Try repeating the information back to the person to be sure you understand what the person is saying.
4. *Take notes to confirm what you are hearing.* Once you have left the person who is speaking, it may be too late to get information. Be sure you write down information while it is fresh in your mind so that there is no misunderstanding later.

Write a sales letter to a friend about one of your favorite products. Remember the object of the letter is to get the reader's attention.

Why is effective listening important for a successful salesperson?
_____
_____

GET THEIR ATTENT ION

Advertising professionals write most sales messages, but it is important for someone in sales to also have good writing skills as you may have to compose a sales letter or informational materials for a customer. Color, catchy slogans, specialty papers, pictures, quotes, and celebrity endorsements are all methods that are used to get the attention of a reader of a sales message. Examples of this would be a golf resort that sends out a sales letter on paper shaped like a golf ball or a movie theater that prints its message on paper that looks like a bucket of popcorn.

SALES LETTER
When writing a sales letter, put yourself in the place of the customer and focus on those things the customer would want to know. A sales letter should emphasize the benefits a customer will receive from the product. Begin a sales letter by getting the reader's attention. Once you have captured the attention of the reader, move to the sales pitch of your letter. Emphasize the features and strengths, not the weaknesses, of the product. The letter should conclude with a request for the reader to take action. If you want the reader to call, include your phone number and a request for a call. If you want him to visit your business, give your address and hours of operation. In order to encourage the reader to act quickly, you might want to put an expiration date on the offer.

Working in a group, make a list of as many companies and their slogans as you can recall.

Be sure your letter is easy to read. Do not make it too long, and be sure it is formatted in an attractive style. If the letter is too long, it may end up in the trash. People are busy and don't have a lot of time to spend on unsolicited mail.

E-MAIL

Companies that use the Internet for sales promotions offer potential customers the opportunity to request more information by e-mail. When these requests

come in, they should be answered promptly and professionally. Maintain a businesslike tone when writing e-mails. Always use complete sentences and proofread carefully. If you are quoting prices, check your figures carefully before sending the e-mail.

E-mail is also a convenient way to contact potential customers with your sales message. It is important that you know your target market well before deciding to use e-mail because many e-mail users block mass mailings and others delete e-mail that is from unknown sources.

Once you have made contact with potential customers, e-mail is often an effective way for you to share information with them and to answer their questions. However, the personal touch is still important in the selling process, so do not depend solely on e-mail for communication.

SALES PROPOSAL

A *sales proposal* is used to offer a product or service to a client. Proposals should be written specifically for a client. Be sure you know whom you are writing for and what the client is looking for before you begin the proposal. If you submit a detailed, technical proposal to someone who is busy and does not have time to go through the material, you will probably lose the sale before you even get in the door. In the proposal, you should show how your product or service can specifically meet the needs of the client.

A sales proposal should be a sample of your best work. If you submit a proposal that is poorly written or has errors, the potential client will not get a good impression of you or the product or service you are trying to sell. Make sure the proposal is formatted attractively, contains correct information, and is error free.

What are some characteristics of a good sales message?

1.3 **COMMUNICATING FOR SUCCESS**

THINK CRITICALLY

1. How is speaking with customers on the telephone similar with meeting them face to face? How is it different?

2. Why should a salesperson develop good listening skills?

3. What are some methods for getting the attention of readers of sales messages?

4. If you received a sales letter addressed to you but your name was misspelled and the letter contained several other errors, what would you think of the company that sent the letter?

5. Why is a well-written sales proposal important?

MAKE CONNECTIONS

6. **COMMUNICATION** Write an e-mail responding to a potential customer who has requested product information on a music CD through your company web site. You may give the customer information on your favorite CD.

7. **RESEARCH** Visit the Internet sites of 10 companies with which you are familiar. Find out if the sites allow you to e-mail the company for information. Make a list of the companies whose Internet sites you visited and list how you can contact them by e-mail.

8. **COMMUNICATION** Find an example of a sales letter. Read the letter and write your reaction to it. Does it get your interest? Does it make you want to know more about the product? What could be done to improve the letter?

9. **COMMUNICATION** Prepare a multimedia sales presentation for an item of your choice that you want to sell to a group of your friends. Present this sales presentation to the class.

REVIEW

CHAPTER SUMMARY

LESSON 1.1 Selling as a Career
A. Selling is a learned art. Any time one person tries to persuade another to do something, selling is taking place. Salespeople often assist customers in making wise buying decisions.

B. There are many career opportunities for salespeople in retail, in manufacturing and wholesale markets, and in financial services. Careers in retail sales as well as in securities, commodities, and financial services sales are predicted to increase between 1998 and 2008.

LESSON 1.2 Attributes for Success
A. A good salesperson is persistent, shows empathy, has integrity, and possesses a high level of product knowledge.

B. In order to achieve a high level of success, a salesperson must be self-motivated and have imagination, patience, and good interpersonal skills.

LESSON 1.3 Communicating for Success
A. Speaking skills—on the telephone, in face-to-face meetings, and in presentations—are important to salespeople. They need to speak clearly and communicate all necessary information to their customers.

B. Good salespeople have excellent listening skills. They need to listen to learn about product information and concerns from customers.

C. Even though most sales messages are written by advertising professionals, salespeople need good writing skills so they can write sales letters and e-mails when necessary.

VOCABULARY BUILDER

Choose the term that best fits the definition. Write the letter of the answer in the space provided. Some terms may not be used.

_____ 1. Explaining how a product or service will benefit your customers and meet their needs

_____ 2. One who returns to shop at a certain business

_____ 3. Merchandise and services are sold to a consumer

_____ 4. Sells products to retailers, industrial firms, government agencies, and other businesses

_____ 5. Sells products to manufacturers or directly to wholesalers or retailers

_____ 6. Works with institutions and individuals who want to invest money

_____ 7. Personality characteristics

a. attributes
b. interpersonal skills
c. manufacturing salesperson
d. repeat customer
e. retail sales
f. sales presentation
g. securities, commodities, and financial service representatives
h. selling
i. wholesaler

CHAPTER 1

REVIEW CONCEPTS

8. Describe the characteristics of someone who is referred to as a "born salesperson."

9. When does selling take place?

10. What makes a customer decide to purchase a product or service?

11. Other than retail sales, where are there career opportunities in sales?

12. Describe the responsibilities of the sales staff in stores that use the personal selling approach?

13. Why is persistence an important attribute for a salesperson?

14. If a salesperson works from home and checks in periodically with a sales manager, is self-motivation necessary? Why or why not?

15. Since many salespeople work individually with customers, why is teamwork important?

REVIEW

16. What are the four tips for effective telephone conversations?
_____
_____
_____

17. Why is it important for a salesperson to be well prepared for meetings and presentations?
_____
_____
_____

18. What can a salesperson find out from listening to customers?
_____
_____

19. Why is it important to proofread letters and e-mails before sending them?
_____
_____

APPLY WHAT YOU LEARNED

20. Name a person whom you consider to be successful in sales. It could be a salesperson you have worked with or someone you have read about. Describe the characteristics the person possesses that you feel have contributed to his or her success.
_____
_____

21. You have learned that integrity is an important attribute for a salesperson. Decide if the salesperson is showing integrity in each of the following situations. Explain your answers.

   a. A pharmaceutical salesperson knows that there is a health risk associated with a new drug that is being introduced on the market but chooses not to share this information with physicians.
   _____

   b. A young mother is interested in a new toy for her 18-month-old baby, but the salesperson informs her that it is not recommended for children under three years of age.
   _____

   c. A real estate salesperson knows that a house for sale is located near a toxic waste dump but neglects to tell a young couple interested in purchasing the house.
   _____

CHAPTER 1

22. Explain the importance of product knowledge for a salesperson. Give an example of a shopping experience you had where the salesperson did or did not have product knowledge and the effect it had on your decision to buy.

_____
_____
_____

23. Do you think your chances of making a sale would be better if you made your initial contact by telephone or in person? Why?

_____
_____
_____

24. Describe some techniques that you could use to become a better listener.

_____
_____
_____

MAKE CONNECTIONS

25. RESEARCH Search the Internet for well-known companies that offer online sales. Browse through the sites and write a brief summary of the type of information you found at the web sites.

26. COMMUNICATION Teamwork is important in sales. You have been asked to motivate your team members to increase their sales by 10 percent in the upcoming year. Prepare a presentation that you will give at the next sales meeting. Present this presentation to your classmates.

27. BUSINESS MATH You work for a company that pays you a 5 percent commission based on your total sales each month. Use a spreadsheet to calculate your commission for each month and your total commission for the first half of the year, the second half of the year, and the entire year. Your monthly sales were:

January	$15,650	July	$15,600
February	$16,785	August	$13,500
March	$12,050	September	$16,890
April	$11,985	October	$19,500
May	$15,600	November	$16,785
June	$14,350	December	$19,990

28. RESEARCH You are helping coworkers prepare for an international business trip. Time is running short and they have not had time to research the business etiquette for the country they will be visiting. Choose a country and research its business etiquette. Prepare a "tip sheet" for your coworkers to refer to when they reach the country so that they will not do anything to offend the clients they will be meeting.

CHAPTER 2

TECHNOLOGY AND SELLING

LESSONS

2.1 TELEMARKETING AND CUSTOMER DATA

2.2 THE INTERNET AND MULTIMEDIA

2.3 USE TECHNOLOGY FOR FOLLOW-UP

CAREERS IN SELLING

CHARLES SCHWAB & CO., INC.

Charles Schwab & Co., Inc., was founded in 1971 in San Francisco. Its mission is to provide customers with the most useful and ethical financial services in the world. Schwab offers a broad range of financial services to individual investors, independent investment managers, retirement plans, and institutions.

An Investment Associate provides sales support by handling both operational and administrative activities. The Investment Associate works with new and existing clients to help them customize their online portfolio on the Schwab.com web site. A bachelor's degree or equivalent work experience and three to five years of experience in the securities or financial services industry is required. The associate must have excellent communication skills and be able to work independently and as part of a team. Thorough understanding of online products and Windows software is also required.

THINK CRITICALLY

1. What about an Investment Associate position appeals to you?
2. Why do you think communication and computer skills are important for this position?

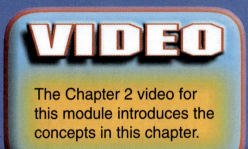

The Chapter 2 video for this module introduces the concepts in this chapter.

PROJECT
Technology and Selling

PROJECT OBJECTIVES
- Explore the role of data collection in sales
- Determine presentation styles that would appeal to a target market
- Recommend activities to follow up sales

GETTING STARTED

Read through the Project Process below. Make a list of any materials you will need. Decide how you will get the needed materials or information.

- You are going to start a business selling used CDs on the Internet. You project that your customers will be young men between the ages of 14 and 20.
- What kind of data would you want to collect from these customers?
- What type of presentation do you think would get their attention?
- Do you think you will need to conduct follow-up activities with customers after they make a purchase?

PROJECT PROCESS

Part 1 LESSON 2.1 Make a list of the data you want to obtain from customers when they make a purchase from the web site.

Part 2 LESSON 2.2 Outline a presentation designed for customers to see when they log onto your web site.

Part 3 LESSON 2.3 Describe any follow-up activities you would conduct after a customer has made a purchase from the web site.

CHAPTER REVIEW

Project Wrap-up Design a form to collect customer data and prepare a multimedia presentation that you could upload onto a web site. Present your form and the presentation to the class. Explain how you would use the data and why you included the information in your presentation.

CHAPTER 2 TECHNOLOGY AND SELLING

LESSON 2.1
TELEMARKETING AND CUSTOMER DATA

GOALS

EXPLORE the role of telemarketing in sales

DETERMINE the role customer data plays in sales

TELEMARKETING

The Direct Marketing Association defines **telemarketing** as the structured use of the telephone to purchase or sell products or services, to obtain or give information to businesses and residences, or to solicit funds or support for charities, political parties, and other nonprofit organizations. Telemarketing has a negative image to many consumers. They think of the unsolicited phone calls that come at dinnertime with a poorly prepared or pushy salesperson on the line unwilling to take "no" for an answer. However, more telemarketing is done business-to-business than business-to-consumer. Did you know that you are participating in telemarketing when you call a catalog company to place an order?

Outbound telemarketing is unsolicited calls made by a company attempting to sell a product. With the increase in postage rates, this is becoming

ON THE $CENE

Yoko Mori works as a sales representative for a company that conducts school fundraisers. Once she meets a teacher, she keeps detailed records about that person, including facts about the teacher's family, hobbies, and other interests. On subsequent visits, she opens her conversation by inquiring about one of the items she has previously learned. What type of impression do you think this makes on the teacher?

2.1 TELEMARKETING AND CUSTOMER DATA

more widely used by businesses. *Inbound* telemarketing allows customers to place orders or request information by calling toll-free or fee-based numbers. Many fee-based numbers use the 900 area code. Since customers have to pay the long-distance charges, the number of calls received may decrease, but the people who do call usually are really interested in the product being offered.

TELEMARKETING USES

As the cost of sales calls continues to rise, telemarketing can be used to save money. Instead of a sales representative calling on smaller accounts, those accounts could be handled by telephone. Or a telemarketer could qualify leads before a sales representative goes on a call. A telephone call often is more effective than a direct-mail advertisement, and unlike companies that use mail, the telemarketing company knows for sure when the call was made and received by the prospect.

THE TELEMARKETING TEAM

The individuals who place and receive calls often will be the first, and perhaps the only, contact a prospect has with your company. It is important for telemarketers to project a positive image for your company. Individuals hired for telemarketing should have a pleasant phone voice and excellent telephone skills and should be articulate and courteous. Training is very important. Telemarketers need a high level of product knowledge and should not sound like they are reading from a script when presenting product information. Telemarketers are better received when they are allowed to present product information using a fact sheet so that they can interact in a more natural manner with customers.

> **did you KNOW?**
>
> In 2000, the average cost of a sales call for a company with a sales force of 10 to 19 sales representatives was $165.02. The average cost of a sales call was highest in the West, with a cost of $232.21, and lowest in the South, with a cost of $146.75.

Telemarketers can play an important role in gathering data, providing personalized attention, and creating lifelong customers for a company. Customer service greatly influences a customer's decision to purchase, and the telemarketing center plays an important part in customer service.

WORKING WITH THE SALES FORCE

By using telemarketers for lead generation and qualification, the time needed to close a sale can be greatly reduced. The telemarketers and the sales force need to work together so that promising leads can be followed up in a timely manner.

LEGISLATIVE REGULATIONS

Many local and state governments as well as the federal government have passed laws dealing with telemarketing. These laws were made in response to complaints about nuisance calls and fraudulent telemarketing. The Telemarketing Sales Rule is a comprehensive regulation that requires specific disclosures, prohibits misrepresentations, limits the times when telemarketers may call customers at their homes, prohibits making calls after a customer has asked not to be called, outlines payment restrictions for the sale of certain goods and services, and requires the maintenance of specific business records.

Explain the role of effective telemarketing.
_____
_____

DATABASE TECHNOLOGY

Sales automation is technology that helps salespeople better manage important account information. This allows salespeople to serve their customers better and enables them to increase sales productivity.

Technology that is available today enables a business to

- Manage customer relationships more effectively
- Generate reports easily
- Plan sales trips effectively
- Share information with other team members immediately
- Trace customer buying needs and schedules
- Provide necessary sales information to customers easily

DATA MANAGEMENT SOFTWARE

Most companies enter the sales automation process by using *contact management software*. This software allows salespeople to keep and use information about their customers and prospects. By recording personal information about the customer, the salesperson is able to establish rapport on subsequent contacts. This software allows salespeople to print sales letters instantly and to track meetings and contacts with clients.

Once a company's salespeople become comfortable using contact management software, they may want to move to *enterprise-wide solutions*, which link the sales force with other departments in the company and give all departments access to the same customer information. All departments work from one centralized

2.1 TELEMARKETING AND CUSTOMER DATA

STAYING IN TOUCH The wireless revolution has enabled salespeople to maintain contact with the home office and customers from anywhere in the world. Some of these wireless "gadgets" allow you to connect to a product database, send a fax from your car, send and receive pager messages and e-mails, transfer schedule information from a computer or an electronic organizer, find driving directions, check stock quotes, retrieve information from and make changes to a company database, use headsets with mobile phones, and transfer images from a computer to a digital picture frame. As technology advances, there will always be new products available to enhance a salesperson's job responsibilities.

THINK CRITICALLY Is it important for a salesperson to keep up with the latest electronic gadgets? Why or why not?

database in an enterprise-wide system. Whenever one user of the system updates client information, all users of the system have access to the updated information.

DATA MINING

Data mining is the process of using automation to detect relevant patterns in a database. This information can be used to create customer profiles and to forecast sales. Data mining also helps determine the reasons for customer loyalty and analyzes the potential return on pricing, promotion, and direct mail strategies. All of this can save a company money and can increase customer loyalty.

Customer Profiles Customer data is an important asset for a company. Once customer data has been gathered, it can be used to save time and enhance the sales process. By storing customer information, including shipping information, method of payment, and items purchased, each time the customer places an order, this information can be accessed and verified, enabling the transaction to be completed more quickly.

Forecast Sales By analyzing data on customer purchases from previous years, a company can see what items are selling best and determine if the time of the year has any impact on sales. This information can be used to decide when inventory needs to be increased on particular items so that customers do not have to wait on backorders. For example, a company that specializes in china and crystal may find that there is a greater demand for its products in the spring and summer as this is a favorite time for weddings to be held.

In small groups, brainstorm to create a list of ways companies can use customer data.

What is the importance of customer data to a company?

THINK CRITICALLY

1. What are some of the uses of telemarketing?

2. What is the difference between inbound and outbound telemarketing?

3. What is the Telemarketing Sales Rule?

4. What is the purpose of data mining?

5. How can analyzing customer data help a company forecast sales?

MAKE CONNECTIONS

6. **RESEARCH** Use the library or Internet to search for information on local, state, or federal legislation dealing with telemarketing regulations. Prepare a presentation about your findings.

7. **COMMUNICATION** If you have never talked with a telemarketer, ask your parents or someone else to describe the experience. If you have talked with a telemarketer, think about the most pleasant or unpleasant experience you had. Write a summary of the call describing what the telemarketer did that was effective and/or ineffective.

8. **RESEARCH** Use the Internet to locate a web site that requires you to register. Make a list of the information the site requests for registration. (You do not have to register at the site.)

9. **RESEARCH** Look through current magazines or on the Internet and find advertisements for electronic gadgets that a salesperson could use. Prepare a poster showing these gadgets and explain what a salesperson would use them for. Present your findings to the class.

2.2 THE INTERNET AND MULTIMEDIA

LESSON 2.2
THE INTERNET AND MULTIMEDIA

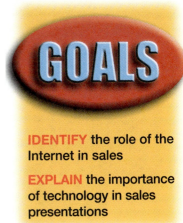

IDENTIFY the role of the Internet in sales

EXPLAIN the importance of technology in sales presentations

INTERNET USAGE

As the Internet is becoming more ingrained in business and personal applications, companies are discovering how the Internet can work for them. Some companies are finding that the Internet is a business tool for improving communication and efficiency while others are finding that it is a good way to attract, acquire, and keep customers. Many companies are also turning to the Internet for sales training. The strength of the Internet is its ability to convey information instantly and accurately. Using the Internet can benefit sales productivity in the following ways.

- more efficient management of resources
- quality management of account information
- timely dissemination of corporate information

ON THE $CENE

Yoko enjoys visiting schools and making presentations to the students about the products they will be selling in the fundraisers. She has a script that she follows, but before she goes to make a presentation, she familiarizes herself with the material so that she does not need the script. She always uses an attention-getting opener and makes sure all students are listening to her before continuing. Sometimes Yoko uses a computerized presentation to highlight the prize program in which the students can participate. Do you think Yoko is well prepared when she goes into the classroom? Why or why not?

- more efficient use of salespeople's time
- better accessibility to sales personnel by the home office and to the home office by salespeople in the field

BUSINESS TOOL

With product and client information stored online in a centralized database, a company can make this information accessible to its salespeople in the field. Information that salespeople can access includes product descriptions, technical specifications, price quotes, and reference sheets. Salespeople can update the home office quickly when they send in their sales data, including account status reports and forecast spreadsheets. Some companies are even making their data available to customers so they can check product information and availability on their own. When a company does this, it must make sure the data is correct and is updated on a regular basis.

Internet versus Intranet When making the decision to go online, a company must decide if it wants to use the Internet or an intranet. The **Internet** is a network of public networks available almost anywhere. An **intranet** is an internal network. The main difference between the two is access. An intranet is designed to be used by a select group, such as employees of a company. To access an intranet, a user must use a dial-up connection to the company's network. An Internet site can be reached through any Internet service provider. Security is an important issue when placing information on the Internet because the site can be accessed by anyone, including competitors and hackers. Some ways to secure data include having a name that is not easily discovered, requiring a password to access a site, and encrypting information.

SALES TRAINING

Using the Internet for sales training is convenient and cost-effective. Sales personnel can access training materials on the Web from any location at a time that is convenient for them. If a company is small and does not have a lot of time to spend training a new sales representative, there are training

BUSINESS ON THE NET

The Internet is breaking down barriers that traditionally limited international business transactions. In order to transact business with people from other countries, a company must be able to conduct business in many different languages. To accommodate Internet users from other countries, a firm may offer versions of its web site in several different languages. The language used on the web site can be changed when the user clicks on a link. This allows Internet users to visit web sites and purchase goods from all over the world.

THINK CRITICALLY What are the advantages for a company placing information in different languages on its web site?

2.2 THE INTERNET AND MULTIMEDIA

programs available online for a small fee. These programs can also be used to update or refresh an existing salesperson's skills.

SELLING ON THE INTERNET

Companies are finding many ways to use the Internet for selling products. Some companies have web sites that allow customers to view product information and then order by phone, mail, or fax. Other companies set up their web sites to allow customers to view product information and then purchase items directly online. And some companies actually are able to deliver products over the Internet.

View Product Information The Internet allows users to get specific information on demand 24 hours a day. One way companies can attract users to their web site is to offer useful information related to the organization's product or service category. For example, a garden shop might have information about plants that will grow in a specific area and how to care for the plants. When Internet users come to the site to read that information, they also find descriptions of products sold at the garden shop.

Place Orders Online For retailers, the biggest challenge in Internet sales is getting customers to their site. It is important for the web site to be registered with search tools such as Yahoo, Highway 61, or Dogpile so that customers will find it when doing a product search. Retailers also need to provide assurances to customers that the credit card data they enter online will be secure. Many web sites use security validation so customers can make their purchases without worrying about the safety of their credit card data.

Many well-known retail stores have launched successful online businesses. Some businesses that are strictly online have thrived while others have not lasted very long. The beginning of the twenty-first century saw a surge of "dot.com" businesses, but by 2001 many of these were gone. Being able to order a product online, allows customers to shop when it is convenient for them. They are not bound by retail operating hours or the location of the store. This makes shopping an easy, timesaving task as opposed to traditional retail shopping. Customers are also able to see immediately if a desired item is available or if an alternate choice needs to be made. Online shopping also allows customers to comparison shop by visiting various web sites offering similar products. Prices can be compared before the decision to buy is made. A web site should include a telephone number that customers can use if they have any problems or questions.

Downloadable Products Downloadable items include magazine subscriptions, software programs, games, music, and books. Customers can visit a web site and, after entering payment information, immediately download and begin using items. This dramatically minimizes customers' wait time.

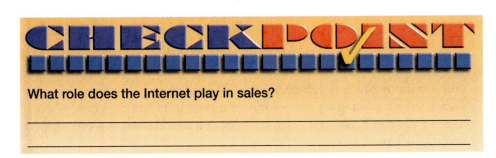

What role does the Internet play in sales?

CHAPTER 2 TECHNOLOGY AND SELLING

Working in small groups, develop a list of ten reasons to use visuals in a sales presentation.

PRESENTATION TECHNOLOGY

Technology has advanced to the point that a salesperson can enter a meeting with a projector and a small computer loaded with presentation software and have all the tools needed for a dynamic, customized presentation. The days of carrying volumes of catalogs and pricing sheets are gone forever. All of this information is now available with the click of a mouse. If a salesperson wants to be competitive, modern technology must be incorporated into the presentation. High-quality presentations that once cost thousands of dollars to produce and usually required assistance from an external production firm now can be done on the laptop computer by a sales representative. The 3M Corporation and the Management Information Systems Research Center found that presentations with visual support are 43 percent more persuasive than those presentations that do not use visual support.

PRESENTATION VISUALS

Use visuals to emphasize and support the main point of a presentation. A well-designed visual aid will help hold the interest of the audience. Use the following tips to create attention-getting and attention-keeping presentations.

- *Use only relevant clip art or pictures.* If you choose graphics that do not support your message, the audience's attention will be lost as they try to find the relevance of the clip art.

- *Be consistent with the use of color throughout the presentation.* Try to stick with two or three main colors that are easily read and that project well.

- *Do not clutter the slide with too much information.* The Rule of Five's states you should have no more than five lines per slide with no more than five words on each line.

- *If you use graphs and charts, be sure they are easy to read and comprehend.* The graphs and charts should be clear and large enough to be seen by the audience.

- *Use a black slide to get your audience's attention off of the slide and onto you.* Software packages have built-in functions that will turn your screen black, and then with a click, will bring the slide back. You might use this feature when making an important point during the presentation. This will cause the viewers to focus all their attention on you.

- *Use the "hide slide" feature to remove slides from the presentation if you are not quite sure whether you will need them.* If you cannot decide before making a presentation, you can "hide" slides. Then, when making the presentation, if you find that you need them, you can simply "unhide" them.

Choose Your Color Carefully

Colors determine the psychological effect your presentation will have on your audience. Use the following guidelines when choosing colors for a presentation.

Red—energy, power, excitement
Orange—happy, confident, creative, adventurous
Yellow—wisdom, playful, satisfying, optimistic
Green—health, regeneration, contentment, harmony
Blue—honesty, integrity, trustworthy
Violet—regal, mystic, beauty, inspiration

2.2 THE INTERNET AND MULTIMEDIA

- ***Put subliminal messages into your presentations by using animation effects.*** You can have messages flash on and off during your presentation. The message can appear for a very brief time and then disappear.

When making the presentation, use the visuals to support what you are saying. Keep your eyes on the audience and do not read from the slides. Practice the presentation until you are comfortable with it and can deliver it in a professional manner. If you would like the audience to have a copy of the material you are presenting, prepare handouts for them. You can easily print copies of your slide presentation with space for viewers to take notes.

AUTOMATED PRESENTATIONS

A product or service presentation can be prepared on the computer and saved on a disk or CD. Audio and video can also be incorporated into the presentation. The presentation then can be used by a salesperson in a face-to-face setting, or it can be set to run automatically and provided to potential customers to view at their leisure. It can also be placed on the Web for individuals to view when browsing your web site.

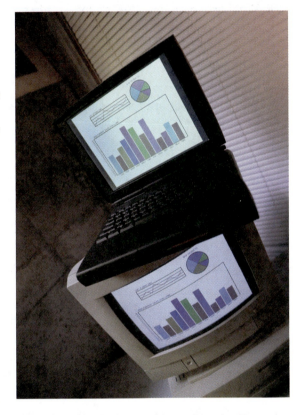

Automated presentations often are run on video displays in trade show booths and kiosks in malls. There, they will run repeatedly for viewing by potential customers as they pass by. Interested viewers can stop and watch more of the presentation as time allows.

CDs can provide an up-close look at a potential product and can reinforce information presented by the sales representative. For example, hotels, resort properties, and cruise lines are using this technology to give customers a virtual tour of the property being considered for a meeting or a vacation.

CHECKPOINT

Why would a salesperson want to use presentation visuals?

_____

_____

THINK CRITICALLY

1. How are businesses using the Internet?

2. What is the difference between the Internet and an intranet?

3. What are three uses for the Internet in selling products?

4. Why is it important for sales presentations to incorporate modern technology?

5. What should you consider when preparing a multimedia presentation?

MAKE CONNECTIONS

6. **RESEARCH** Using the Internet, search for sites that sell products online. Make a list of the companies and identify each of them as being strictly an online business or a traditional retailer with an online site.

7. **COMMUNICATION** You are working as a member of the sales team for your school. Your mission is to encourage all students in your district to choose your school over other schools in the area. Outline the features of your school that you would include in a presentation to be viewed in a kiosk in the local shopping mall. Design a multimedia presentation of the features. Choose a color scheme representative of your school and add appropriate graphics to the presentation.

8. **COMMUNICATION** Interview a business owner who has a web site. Find out what made him or her decide to start the web site and what the primary purpose is for having the web site. Ask if the use of the web site has changed since it was first launched. Prepare a report of your findings. Present the report to your class.

LESSON 2.3
USE TECHNOLOGY FOR FOLLOW-UP

EXPLORE the role of technology in getting the product to the customer after the sale

DESCRIBE the role of technology in providing customer assistance after the sale is made

FULFILLMENT

Once a customer has placed an order, the next step is **fulfillment**, the delivery of merchandise promptly, accurately, and in good condition. To the customer, this is the most important step. The customer is not concerned with how the order is processed or who packs it in the warehouse. All the customer cares about is receiving the order in a timely manner. And with increased use of the Internet for ordering, customers expect even faster delivery of products. Therefore, it is important for a business to have adequate inventory on hand so that orders can be filled when placed. As a salesperson, you will want to be sure that your customers are pleased with all the service they receive from your company.

ON THE $CENE

Once Yoko receives an order from a school, she immediately writes a thank you note to anyone involved with organizing the fundraiser. She then uses her company's order-tracking software to track the order as it moves through the fulfillment process. A couple of days before the order is to be delivered, she contacts the school to alert them that the order is coming. She also follows up a few days later to see if there are any problems with the order. What do you think the teachers think about Yoko's follow-up activities? If there are problems with the order, how do you think you should handle the situation?

CHAPTER 2 TECHNOLOGY AND SELLING

NINE STEPS TO FULFILLMENT

Fulfillment has been described as having nine major steps. Those steps include:

1. ***Order forms and instructions*** When an order is placed in person, this step may be completed by the salesperson. Orders made online include selecting merchandise, transferring it to an online shopping cart, and filling out shipping information.

2. ***Order receipt*** Orders can be received by mail, fax, telephone, online, or in person. This step includes the processing and data entry of the order.

3. ***Credit approval*** This includes credit card authorization or check clearance.

4. ***Data mining*** In this step, customer data is collected for marketing purposes.

5. ***Inventory control*** Merchandise should always be available, but levels of stock should not be kept too high.

6. ***Billing*** This involves the production of the initial bill, if the order has not been pre-paid, and any necessary follow-up reminders.

7. ***Reports*** Marketing, merchandising, operating, and financial control reports are produced.

8. ***Order filling and shipping*** Products are received, stocked, picked, packed, and shipped.

9. ***Customer service*** Inquiries, complaints, and returns of merchandise are handled.

BUSINESS MATH CONNECTION

Invoices are prepared for customers so they know how much they owe. Many invoices are prepared electronically, but you may be asked to check an invoice or calculate the amount of a sale for a customer. Calculate the selling price by multiplying the unit cost by the number of items purchased. Mid-Carolina Computers purchased 3 computer monitors @ $320 each and 2 color printers @ $299 each. What is the total cost of the merchandise? (The @ symbol represents "at" and is commonly used on invoices.)

SOLUTION
To calculate the total cost, multiply the quantity ordered times the unit price for each item. Then add those amounts together.

$3 \times \$320 = \$960$
$2 \times \$299 = \$598$
$\$960 + \$598 = \$1,558$

The total cost to Mid-Carolina Computers is $1,558.

2.3 USE TECHNOLOGY FOR FOLLOW-UP

SALESPERSON'S ROLE IN FULFILLMENT

The salesperson can play a vital role in the steps of the fulfillment process. Throughout the process, there are opportunities for the salesperson to make contact with the customers to keep them informed and to check on their satisfaction. Technology has enabled the salesperson to be involved with the process without spending a great amount of time on it.

COMPUTER TECHNOLOGY

The computer technology of a company will have an effect on its ability to handle order fulfillment. There are software packages that can help with every step of the fulfillment process. However, if the company's software is not adequate, it can hinder the process.

For example, computer-generated reports can help a company see which products are in demand and which products are slow to move, so the technology can assist in inventory control. On the other hand, when computer technology is not adequate, it can result in long delays. Long delays lead to frustration on the part of online shoppers and, thus, fewer orders.

WORKSHOP

Working in small groups, discuss online experiences you have had with a web site where you had problems because the company's technology was inadequate.

CHECKPOINT

What role does technology play in the fulfillment process?

_____
_____

THE PERSONAL TOUCH

Successful selling is all about **repeat business**—when a customer returns to your business for a subsequent purchase. The steps you take after a sale are just as important to the customer as the steps leading up to the sale. If you want to build a sales relationship with a customer, take time to follow up as the product is delivered and used. As a salesperson, technology can assist you in the follow-up process.

Using computer software, you can **track** or follow the progress of an order through the fulfillment process. Immediately after the order is placed, send an e-mail or a card thanking the customer for the order. Continue tracking the order's progress and delivery. Just before delivery, e-mail or call to let the customer know delivery is pending. The customer will appreciate the notification, especially if the item is large and the customer needs to make space for it, or if it is perishable and the customer needs to have someone present to accept delivery.

Once delivery is complete, it is a good practice to check with the customer again by phone or e-mail to see if everything was received in good condition and to be certain that there are no problems. Make sure your customers understand that their satisfaction is your main concern.

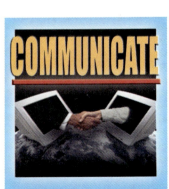

COMMUNICATE

Compose an e-mail that you could send to a customer who just placed a large order with you.

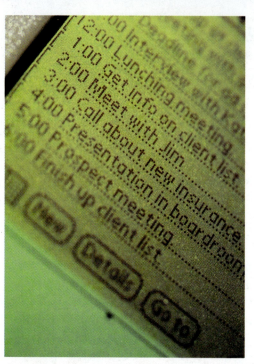

PERSONAL ORGANIZER

Use a computer organizer or personal organizer to note when delivery of the product was made and make a notation for your software to notify you two months after that date. If you do not hear from customers during that time, contact them when you get the reminder. Ask if you can be of any service to them or if they have any questions or problems.

ONLINE CUSTOMER ASSISTANCE

Through a company web site there are several ways to offer assistance to customers. These include order tracking, FAQs, instructional materials, and chat rooms.

Order Tracking Using their assigned order number, customers can log in and track the progress of their order until it is delivered. This allows customers to check on their order when it is convenient for them. It also eliminates the waiting time involved in a telephone call.

Frequently Asked Questions Questions about a product that are commonly asked by customers are called **FAQs**. These questions and their answers are placed online, and customers can often find an answer to a question just by looking on the web site.

Instructional Material Many times, a customer will lose or damage a product's instructional manual and will need a replacement copy. Having a copy online that customers can reference or download can save a great deal of time and frustration. It also eliminates the wait time for the manual when sent by regular mail.

Chat Rooms Many company web sites will set up a chat room for customers to use to share their experiences about a product. Oftentimes, customers may discover something about their product that they did not previously know. These chat rooms are common on the web sites of luxury car dealers and manufacturers, and car owners can use them to share information about their car with other owners.

How can technology aid a salesperson in providing customer assistance after the sale?

___
___

THINK CRITICALLY

1. Why is fulfillment so important to a business?
   _____
   _____
   _____
   _____

2. Explain how technology can affect the fulfillment process.
   _____
   _____
   _____
   _____

3. What things can be done after a sale to encourage customers to return to your business for future sales?
   _____
   _____
   _____
   _____

4. How can a salesperson use a personal organizer to assist with follow-up after a sale?
   _____
   _____
   _____
   _____

5. What types of online customer assistance can be made available on a web site?
   _____
   _____
   _____
   _____

MAKE CONNECTIONS

6. **RESEARCH** Visit the Internet site of a company that sells a product and has a FAQ section. Read through the questions and answers on the site. Summarize the information that you learned about the product from the FAQs.

7. **RESEARCH** Choose one of your favorite products. Think of questions a new user of the product might have. Prepare FAQs that could be posted on the product's web site.

8. **BUSINESS MATH** You are a salesperson at a small bookstore and coffee shop. Design a spreadsheet to calculate the total cost for orders. Calculate the total cost for a customer who purchased the following:

   3 CDs @ $17.99 each
   4 books @ $14.95 each
   1 magazine @ $5.25
   2 cups of specialty coffee @ $2.95 each

REVIEW

CHAPTER SUMMARY

LESSON 2.1 Telemarketing and Customer Data
A. Telemarketing is widely used in business-to-business sales and is often more effective than direct mail. For telemarketers to represent their company well, they need a high level of product knowledge and excellent communication and telephone skills.

B. Technology allows all employees of a company to have access to customer and product data. This is important to sales representatives in the field as they can immediately access product information and update order information when making a sales call.

LESSON 2.2 The Internet and Multimedia
A. The Internet is a business tool for improving communication and efficiency, and it can also be used to attract customers. Companies are using the Internet to provide sales training to their sales staff and to provide product information, take orders, and sell downloadable products to their customers.

B. Technology allows salespeople to present all clients with customized presentations that in the past would have been used only for major clients.

LESSON 2.3 Use Technology for Follow-Up
A. Once a sale is made, it is important for a company to focus on getting the product to the customer in a timely manner. Technology can play a major role throughout the fulfillment process.

B. Technology provides easy methods for a salesperson to stay in touch with the customer throughout the sales process. A company can also offer customers assistance on its web site. A happy customer is more likely to return for subsequent purchases.

VOCABULARY BUILDER

Choose the term that best fits the definition. Write the letter of the answer in the space provided. Some terms may not be used.

_____ 1. Structured use of the telephone to purchase or sell products or services

_____ 2. Technology that helps salespeople better manage account information

_____ 3. Follow the progress of an order

_____ 4. Network of public networks available almost anywhere

_____ 5. Internal network

_____ 6. Delivery of merchandise promptly, accurately, and in good condition

_____ 7. When a customer returns to your business for a subsequent purchase

_____ 8. Questions commonly asked by customers about a product

a. data mining
b. FAQs
c. fulfillment
d. Internet
e. intranet
f. repeat business
g. sales automation
h. telemarketing
i. track

CHAPTER 2

REVIEW CONCEPTS

9. Why does telemarketing have a negative image with many people?

10. Why is training for a telemarketer important for success in sales?

11. How can telemarketers assist the sales force?

12. Why did governments at the local, state, and federal levels enact laws regulating telemarketing?

13. How does sales automation assist salespeople?

14. What is the difference between contact management software and enterprise-wide solutions?

15. What type of information can salespeople in the field access from a centralized database?

16. What are the advantages to a company using online training programs?

REVIEW

17. How has technology affected sales presentations?

18. Summarize the nine steps in the fulfillment process.

19. How can the reports prepared in the fulfillment process be used?

20. Which step of the fulfillment process is most important to the customer?

21. Why is repeat business important to a company?

22. When following up with customers, why should you make sure that your customers understand that you are concerned with their satisfaction?

APPLY WHAT YOU LEARNED

23. Describe a telemarketing call you have received at your home. Tell what the telemarketer did well and how the caller could improve.

24. As a consumer, how do you feel about a company storing data about you when you purchase from them?

CHAPTER 2

25. What is the purpose of a subliminal message in a sales presentation? Do you think they should be used? Why or why not?
_____
_____

26. Why is follow-up by a salesperson an important part of the sales process?
_____
_____

27. Why should a company provide customer follow-up by telephone as well as online?
_____
_____

28. Why would a company want to monitor the conversations that go on in a chat room that the company provides for customers?
_____
_____

MAKE CONNECTIONS

29. **RESEARCH** Search the Internet for a site that features an online presentation. Try the AT&T, Ford Motor Company, or Microsoft web sites. Write a critique of the presentation using the guidelines for presentations in Lesson 2.2.

30. **COMMUNICATION** Work with a partner to create a presentation on the use of the Internet for selling. You may use the information in your text and other resources. Follow the guidelines in your text for creating an effective presentation. Present this presentation to your classmates.

31. **BUSINESS MATH** Use a spreadsheet to prepare an invoice for Alternative Apparel, 200 Oakbrook Parkway, Atlanta, GA 30303, for the following items:

    288 white cotton t-shirts @ $2.99 each

    12 dozen blue baseball hats @ $36.00 per dozen

    144 white aprons @ $3.45 each

    576 blue and white golf shirts @ $4.25 each

    Because Alternative Apparel is a wholesaler, no sales tax is charged. Alternative Apparel pays shipping charges to the delivery company.

32. **COMMUNICATION** Working as a salesperson, you frequently send thank you letters to customers after they have made a purchase from you. In order to save time, you decide to use word processing software to prepare a generic letter that you can customize for customers after each sale. Write the copy for the body of this letter.

CHAPTER 3

PREPARING TO SELL

LESSONS

3.1 PSYCHOLOGY OF SELLING

3.2 KNOWLEDGE FOR SELLING

3.3 PROSPECTING FOR SALES

CAREERS IN SELLING

BORDERS, INC.

With nearly 300 stores worldwide, Borders, founded in 1971, has developed a reputation as a store where customers can rely on friendly, well-informed staff and a diverse inventory of books and music.

One job that prepares employees for career advancement is In-Store Corporate Sales Representative (CSR). The CSR develops, maintains, and drives sales for businesses and institutions. Job responsibilities include servicing accounts, tracking and reporting sales, maintaining account files, and meeting monthly sales goals. Store responsibilities include researching prices and availability of titles, communicating orders from management to clerks, and handling customer orders and service issues.

For the CSR position, Borders looks for a person who has a background in business and previous sales experience. The person should be able to handle multi-faceted projects and utilize creative problem-solving skills. Experience with Microsoft Word and Excel programs is also preferred.

THINK CRITICALLY
1. What personal skills would you need to be a successful CSR?
2. What are the advantages of Borders' policy to promote from within to the store and its employees?

The Chapter 3 video for this module introduces the concepts in this chapter.

PROJECT
Preparing to Sell

PROJECT OBJECTIVES
- Explore the benefits and features of a product
- Determine the needs that the product will meet for customers
- Explore the best way to work with customers based on their behavior traits

GETTING STARTED

Read through the Project Process below. Make a list of any materials you will need. Decide how you will get the needed materials or information.
- Form small groups and choose a product that your group would like to sell.
- Find out who makes the product and where the product is currently sold.
- Discuss what customer needs the product satisfies.

PROJECT PROCESS

Part 1 **LESSON 3.1** Using the product you have chosen, develop a sales and marketing strategy worksheet. This is the information with which you would need to be very familiar if you were going to sell this product. For this part, answer the following questions: Who would buy the product and why? What needs could be met by purchasing this product?

Part 2 **LESSON 3.2** Continue developing your sales and marketing strategy worksheet by answering the following questions: What are the benefits to the customer in purchasing this product? What evidence of the features would convince a customer that your claims about the product are true? Who makes this product? What are the features of this product that make it better than competing products?

Part 3 **LESSON 3.3** Now that you have developed a sales and marketing strategy, you are ready to begin the sales process. You need to think about the type of behavioral traits your customer has. Choose one of the behavioral types in Lesson 3.3 and describe the way you would work with someone possessing these traits.

CHAPTER REVIEW

Project Wrap-up Using the information you developed in Parts 1 and 2, develop a "Sales and Marketing Strategy Information Sheet" for this product that you could give to salespeople to study before they go on a sales call. With a partner, role play an approach to the behavioral type that you described in Part 3.

CHAPTER 3 PREPARING TO SELL

LESSON 3.1
PSYCHOLOGY OF SELLING

DETERMINE how needs affect the personal selling process

EXPLORE the role of relationship selling in the personal selling process

PERSONAL SELLING

Personal selling is direct communication between a sales representative and one or more prospective buyers who attempt to influence each other in a purchase situation. In personal selling, the salesperson must take time to uncover and identify the customer's needs, issues, and concerns. Once they have been determined, the salesperson can sell to meet these needs.

WHAT CUSTOMERS WANT

Salespeople often describe what they are selling in terms of **features**, physical characteristics or capabilities. However, customers want **benefits**, the advantages that could result from features. A successful salesperson will always stress the benefits of products or services to the customer. Knowing the

ON THE $CENE

Maria is enjoying her new job as a sales representative for a beauty supply company. Since she does not have to report to an office each morning, she stays out late at night, sleeps in, and makes her first sales call most days around 1 or 2 p.m. She gets in her car and drives until she finds a beauty salon, and then she goes in and asks to speak to the manager. Sometimes she realizes she has spoken to that manager on a previous visit. What advice would you give Maria about her work habits?

3.1 PSYCHOLOGY OF SELLING

benefits will give customers reasons to buy at the asking price. If the customer does not perceive value in the product or service you are selling, it will be easier for the customer to object to the price later in the sales process.

BUYING MOTIVES

When you approach a soft drink machine, insert money, and receive a drink, you do this to satisfy a need. The need is for a drink because you are thirsty, and the drink quenches your thirst. As a salesperson, you will need to determine what *motivates* or makes a person decide to buy. **Maslow's Hierarchy of Needs** arranges needs in ascending order of importance: physiological needs, safety or security needs, social needs, esteem needs, and self-actualization needs. Understanding which need a person is trying to meet will help you explain the benefits of the product or service to that person.

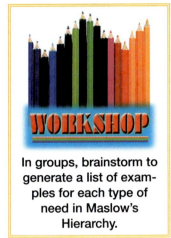

In groups, brainstorm to generate a list of examples for each type of need in Maslow's Hierarchy.

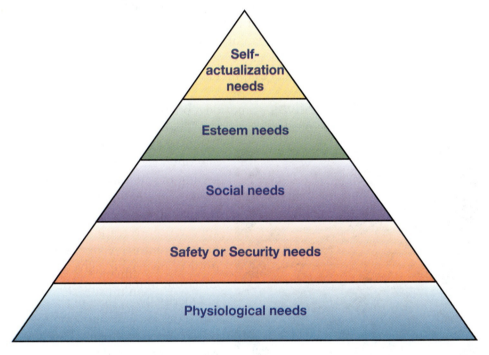

Physiological Needs   The most basic needs are the physiological needs for food, water, and shelter. These needs must be satisfied before an individual can move to a higher-level need.

Safety or Security Needs   Safety or security needs include the need for physical and mental security, economic security, and protection from harm and physical illness. Once the physiological needs are met, safety needs emerge.

Social Needs   Social needs result from a person's desire to be accepted. Social acceptance comes as a result of moving up the Needs Hierarchy. Goals at this level include love and friendship. In a business environment, an individual trying to fill a social need will look for friendly associates and a company with a reputation of being a good place to work.

Esteem Needs   Esteem needs are met by being accepted for contributions made to a group. People seek the feeling of importance when they are filling an esteem need. Esteem needs are satisfied in business by giving individuals titles, sending letters of appreciation, and presenting awards.

49

Self-actualization Needs Self-actualization needs result from a desire within all of us to reach our ultimate level of potential. Maslow felt that most people never reach this level because they are working so hard to achieve lower-level goals.

SATISFACTION OF NEEDS

According to Maslow, workers are motivated by the lowest level of need that is unmet at a particular time. This also would be true for consumers. Lower-level needs are probably not motivators to use in personal selling situations because many of these needs will be met through *transaction selling*, the exchange of a product or service for the purchase price or the promise to pay the purchase price. A salesperson using the personal selling approach should concentrate on satisfying upper-level needs.

Rational Buying Motives Rational buying decisions are based on the customers' logical reasoning. The most popular rational buying motives include safety, simplicity, quality, reliability, economy, convenience, service, durability, knowledge, money gain, and ease of operation. Rational customers will evaluate their options and make a purchase only after they have given it careful thought.

Emotional Buying Motives Emotional buying motives are based on the desire to have a specific product or service. Customers buy specific items

because of their personal feelings and often act on impulse. Most buying motives are emotional. Some of the emotional buying motives include fear, protection, appearance, recreation, improved health, comfort, recognition, pride of ownership, adventure, affection, imitation, prestige, and popularity. Even though these purchases are based on emotions, buyers perceive the purchase as a way to fill real needs. So, they like to justify their purchase decisions rationally. When buyers make a purchase based on an emotional motive, the salesperson should present logical reasons for them to use to justify the purchase.

CHECKPOINT ✓

How is the personal selling process used to satisfy needs?

3.1 PSYCHOLOGY OF SELLING

RELATIONSHIP SELLING

Traditional personal selling approaches attempted to get buyers to accept a point of view or persuade them to take some action. Once the salesperson had the buyer somewhat convinced, he tried to trick, persuade, or coerce the customer to buy. This approach is used less by professional salespeople today as they are turning to **relationship selling**, which emphasizes the relationship between a salesperson and buyer. Today customers are more sophisticated and demand higher levels of customer service. They want someone they can trust who understands their needs and wants. Relationship selling meets these needs. In relationship selling, the salesperson gets to know customers very well, becomes a problem solver for them, and strives to build long-term relationships with them by developing trust over time. Instead of a product or service, the focus becomes the selling of advice and assistance. The salesperson works with customers to develop solutions.

According to a survey by *Purchasing* magazine, the number one dislike among buyers is sellers' lack of preparation, followed closely by lack of interest or purpose.

CUSTOMER KNOWLEDGE

In relationship selling, the salesperson must spend time with customers without the expectation of making a sale every time. The customers' needs are the focus in relationship selling, so time spent learning about a potential customer is an important part of relationship building. Some of the things you should discover before your initial meeting with a prospective customer include the following.

- Where the prospect is currently purchasing the type of product or service you are selling
- How purchasing decisions are made at the prospect's company
- Whether anyone from your company has previously called on the prospective customer
- Whether the prospect's company has ever bought from your company, and if it has, why it didn't continue to purchase from you
- How long the prospect has been with his or her company

BUILD TRUST

In order to build trust with customers, you should take time to let the customer get to know you as a person. You should allow time for small talk with customers, and be sure they know why you believe in the product or service you are selling. Pay close attention to the details in selling and working with your customers.

Always keep your word because it can be one of your most powerful sales tools. If an order is not going to be delivered when promised, communicate with the customer, let him or her know what you are doing to solve the problem, and see what you can do to lessen the inconvenience.

COMMUNICATE

Compose a list of open-ended questions to ask an auto dealer to learn who presently supplies the stereo systems it installs in new cars when buyers do not want a factory-installed system.

FOCUS ON FILLING CUSTOMERS' NEEDS

When customers know you care about what they want and need, they will feel they are making the right decision in buying from you. When you have clearly identified the needs of your customers, you can confirm whether they are part of your target market. You may not have a product to meet a particular need, but you can build trust and a chance for a future relationship with them if you refer them to a more suitable resource.

ASK OPEN-ENDED QUESTIONS

Open-ended questions that require more than a "yes" or "no" answer are used to acquire information from a customer. Follow the traditional "who, what, when, where, why, and how" interviewing technique when gathering information. When you ask customers questions, reply to their responses by linking key product or service benefits to the customer's requirements. Examples of yes or no questions are given below. Each question is then given as an open-ended question.

Yes or No Question	Open-ended Question
Do you need help?	How can I help you?
Do you like the product you are currently using?	What do you like and dislike about the product you are using?
Have you ever tried our product?	Why haven't you tried our product?
Will you be available to meet with me this week?	When and where can I meet with you this week?

LISTEN MORE THAN YOU TALK

Listening is an important skill for a salesperson. When you listen more than you talk, your customers realize that you are really interested in them and that you are trying to understand their specific situation. Customers will feel more comfortable with you and realize that you are on their side.

It is possible to train yourself to be a better listener. Try applying the following tactics.

- Stop talking
- Look at the customer
- Leave your emotions behind
- Avoid jumping to conclusions and making judgments
- Focus on the main points the customer is making

Why should a salesperson ask open-ended questions?

_____

_____

3.1 PSYCHOLOGY OF SELLING

THINK CRITICALLY

1. What are the five levels of needs defined in Maslow's Hierarchy of Needs?

2. What is transaction selling?

3. What is the difference between a rational buying decision and an emotional buying decision?

4. What types of things should a salesperson try to find out about a customer?

5. What things can a salesperson do to build a relationship with a customer?

MAKE CONNECTIONS

6. **RESEARCH** Shop at a store where the personal selling approach is used. Write a brief report on how the salesperson handled the sales process.

7. **COMMUNICATION** Make a list of ten items you have purchased recently. Describe the need you were satisfying when you purchased each item.

8. **COMMUNICATION** Prepare a presentation on relationship selling that could be used for training a new salesperson. Present the presentation to your class.

9. **PROBLEM SOLVING** You have been hired as a salesperson at a luxury car dealership. Most customers will be satisfying an emotional buying motive when purchasing a car from you, but they would like to be able to rationalize their purchase. Choose a luxury car model and find a list of the features of the car that could serve as a rationalization for the customer to purchase the car.

53

CHAPTER 3 PREPARING TO SELL

LESSON 3.2
KNOWLEDGE FOR SELLING

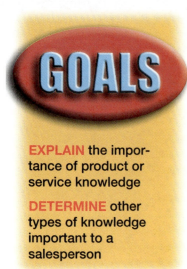

GOALS

EXPLAIN the importance of product or service knowledge

DETERMINE other types of knowledge important to a salesperson

PRODUCT OR SERVICE KNOWLEDGE

To be successful at selling a product or service, a salesperson must have thorough knowledge of the product or service. The two aspects of product knowledge are *features* and *benefits*.

Features are the physical characteristics or capabilities of a product or service. Benefits are the advantages that could result from features of the product or service. Features are discussed as the product or service is presented while benefits are explained in identifying the product or service's ability to solve the customer's problems. Both should be included when presenting a product or service to a potential customer. Presenting features without benefits leads the potential customer to question the price. Presenting benefits without features is the practice of a con person who makes lots of promises with nothing to back them up.

ON THE $CENE

Maria sells a wide range of products for the beauty supply company. When she started her job, the company sent her to several workshops and provided her with a lot of product literature to read. They wanted her to learn all about the products she would be selling. However, Maria never found time to read the product literature and really did not concentrate on the speakers and videos at the workshop. Do you think Maria was prepared for her sales calls?

3.2 KNOWLEDGE FOR SELLING

GLOBAL SALES SUCCESS

In order to expand into other countries and develop a global presence, a company's whole approach to doing business must be modified to meet the country's needs. To truly be international, a company needs more than an office in another country. Products and services must be globally and culturally adapted to be successful. A sales process must be developed that can be customized to work within different countries and cultures. Native sales representatives will be better suited to working in the country than non-natives. All representatives should have consistent training, and training should be done in their native language.

THINK CRITICALLY What advantages does a company have in training natives to be a part of its sales force in other countries?

WHAT'S IN IT FOR ME?

The salesperson who attracts a prospective customer's attention is the one who does the best job explaining how that customer will benefit from a product or service. In many sales presentations, benefits are never mentioned by the salesperson. It is assumed that the customer will be able to determine the benefits from the features presented. This does not usually happen, and a sales opportunity may be lost because the customer did not see the benefits in making the purchase.

When contacting a customer for the first time, you should use a **general benefit strategy** that tells the customer

- Who you are
- Whom you represent (the name of your company)
- What you do
- What you can do for the customer

This strategy will increase your chances of a successful first contact with the customer. If you give the customer a reason to meet with you and create value in the customer's mind, you are establishing a foundation on which to build a future sales call.

EVIDENCE OF FEATURES

A salesperson should present evidence to a prospective buyer about the features and benefits of the product or service being sold. Evidence comes in many forms.

Expertise Expertise is the opinion of experts. A salesperson can become an expert in the field by building a reputation over time or by earning certification in the field. An example of this would be an insurance underwriter who earns the title of Certified Life Underwriter (CLU).

WORKSHOP

Working in groups, brainstorm to develop a list of advertisements in magazines, newspapers, and on television that have famous people providing testimonials for a product. Discuss why you think the company chose that person to represent its product.

Numerical Data If you have numerical data that proves a point about your product or service, share it with the prospective customer. Check these figures often so that you do not report out-of-date information.

Tests To prove claims about a product, testing can be helpful. The tests should be simple to conduct and should always produce the same results. If possible, the prospective customer should be allowed to conduct the tests.

Guarantee A well-known company can offer a *guarantee*, a promise about the quality of the product or service. The salesperson should review everything that is covered in the guarantee with the prospective customer.

Case Histories Salespeople often document instances where using their product or service was worthwhile for a company. Likewise, they also document instances where failure to use their product or service was damaging to a company in some way. If the salesperson feels that a prospective customer would positively relate to the experiences of others, case histories can be helpful evidence.

Testimonials A testimonial is a first-person case history. Often, satisfied customers will allow prospective customers to contact them with questions. They may even offer to help the salesperson by writing a personal letter to a prospective customer stating what the product or service has done for them.

Why is product or service knowledge important to a salesperson?

_____
_____

OTHER NECESSARY KNOWLEDGE

In addition to knowledge of the customer and the product or service, a successful salesperson should also have knowledge of the industry, the market, the company, and the competition.

KNOWLEDGE OF THE INDUSTRY

An **industry** is a particular group of businesses with similar products. In order to be successful as a salesperson, you must understand the basic operations of the industry in which you are selling. Ways to gain industry knowledge include reading *industry* or *trade* publications, studying industry outlook projections and trends, and being involved with industry insiders.

KNOWLEDGE OF THE MARKET

The market consists of the potential buyers to whom the firm can sell. This market is then divided into territories for the firm's salespeople. In addition to learning about the market or potential customers, the salesperson needs to learn about the external forces that affect the prospective customers'

3.2 KNOWLEDGE FOR SELLING

BUSINESS MATH CONNECTION

Deciding what to charge for a product is very important in selling. Because most businesses keep records in terms of retail dollars, the retail method of marking up merchandise is a widely used method of pricing. The initial markup is expressed as a percentage of the unknown retail selling price. To calculate the retail price, subtract the markup percentage from 100 percent and divide it into the cost. If a shirt costs $60 and the desired initial markup is 30 percent, what would the retail price be?

SOLUTION

Retail Price = Cost ÷ (100% − Markup)
Retail Price = $60 ÷ (1.00 − 0.30)
Retail Price = $60 ÷ 0.70

The retail price of the shirt would be $85.71.

decisions. These external forces include legal constraints, technology, customs, attitudes, economic conditions, and expectations.

KNOWLEDGE OF THE COMPANY

The sales force serves as a link between the company and the customers. It is essential that the sales force understand all aspects of the company's operations since they affect the buyer either directly or indirectly.

Departments must communicate and know what the other departments are doing. If the sales department does not know what promotions the marketing department is sending out, then salespeople can appear unprepared to a customer. The shipping department has to understand the delivery schedules that salespeople are promising. When customers call the customer service department, they should get a response that is in line with what the salesperson promised them. If the company does not provide this training for you, then you should take initiative to learn about the company's operations.

KNOWLEDGE OF THE COMPETITION

As a salesperson, you must have knowledge of the products or services sold by your company, and about those sold by your competition. Your customers probably are familiar with competitors' products and may even own some. You need to know the strengths and weaknesses of the competition's products or services so you can sell the benefits and features of yours in comparison to theirs. To gain competitive knowledge, a salesperson can shop the competition, read trade journals, and talk to customers.

Other than customer and product knowledge, what types of knowledge must a salesperson have to be successful?

THINK CRITICALLY

1. Why are both benefits and features important in a sales presentation?

2. What is the purpose of a general benefit strategy?

3. What are three types of evidence that could be presented to a prospective customer?

4. Why is it important for sales representatives to have a thorough knowledge of the company for which they work?

5. How can a salesperson learn about the competition?

MAKE CONNECTIONS

6. **RESEARCH** Look through advertisements in magazines and newspapers for evidence of features that use expertise, numerical data, tests, or guarantees. Prepare a poster of the information you find.

7. **RESEARCH** Choose a type of business in your area. Using the Internet or Yellow Pages, make a list of the names and addresses of all companies in the industry you have chosen. Mark the locations of the companies on a map. Make a list of the companies in the same market that probably compete with each other.

8. **BUSINESS MATH** Use a spreadsheet to calculate the retail price of each of the following items.

Item	Cost	Markup on Retail	Retail Price
Slacks	$32.00	45%	
Shoes	$36.00	60%	
Sweater	$28.00	55%	

LESSON 3.3
PROSPECTING FOR SALES

GOALS

IDENTIFY methods used for prospecting

IDENTIFY behavioral qualities of the four prospect styles

SEARCHING FOR CUSTOMERS

As a successful salesperson, you will look for potential customers whenever, wherever, and however you can find them. Communicating to everyone what you do and the problems you solve is essential to finding prospective customers. **Prospecting** is the process of searching for individuals who qualify as potential customers for the product or service you are selling. Prospective customers will come from the field that is made up of all people and organizations in your assigned territory. There are two different methods for prospecting—the blind search and the selective search.

BLIND SEARCH

The **blind search** is a random attempt to find and identify potential customers. In a blind search, no criteria are used to qualify contacts. Efforts are directed toward everyone in the field.

ON THE $CENE

Maria is under pressure from her sales manager to increase her sales. She has not been making sales at the salons she has been calling on and really does not know where to go next. She has talked to her friend Sergio about her problem. Sergio, a successful computer software salesman, told Maria she needs to search for some prospects. He suggested she start with the Yellow Pages. Can you recommend any other places for Maria to search for customers?

Door-to-Door Sales Door-to-door sales is one type of blind search for prospective customers. Salespeople knock on every door in an area looking for prospective customers. Magazine subscriptions or candy sales are examples of door-to-door sales that you may have encountered. This can be a time-consuming and often discouraging method of prospecting. Most salespeople will not enjoy this type of work for an extended period of time.

Media Advertising Although not commonly used for prospecting, media advertising in print and broadcast formats is used in some situations. Ads in local newspapers and trade magazines are used to seek a direct response from prospective customers. Some of the industries that use this approach include real estate, automobile, and insurance companies. A radio or television advertisement that asks prospective customers to call for more information is another method of a blind search. The names of individuals who call are divided among the sales force for follow-up.

Telemarketing Telemarketing, which was discussed in Chapter 2, is another blind search method. Telephone calls placed to everyone in the field usually bring few leads, but the low cost of this type of person-to-person contact makes this a popular search method for many companies. Telemarketing can be handled in-house or outsourced to telemarketing companies.

SELECTIVE SEARCH

The **selective search** includes any prospecting method that is not random. Generally, a selective search produces better results than a blind search. In a selective search, selection criteria are applied before contacts are made. With a selective search, your audience should be as specific as your message.

Personal Observation A salesperson must always be on the lookout for prospective customers. The opportunity to make a sale is not confined to any particular place or time. Watching a local news show, reading the daily newspaper, and attending events in your community all could bring about opportunities for selling.

3.3 PROSPECTING FOR SALES

Referrals Any name given to you by another person is a referral. Satisfied customers are the best source of referrals. The *center-of-influence* referral method involves cultivating a relationship with an individual who can supply you with the names of many prospective customers. For example, a homebuilder may give an interior designer the names of individuals who are building new homes and might need assistance with decorating.

Use your best customers to find more people like them who may have a similar need for the same product or service you offer. Be sure to identify your most profitable customers when using the center-of-influence referral method.

Working in a group, make a list of as many individuals as you can who could be a center-of-influence for someone else in a selling position.

Asking for a Referral

When asking for a referral, here are some tips to keep in mind.

- Ask for one name at a time.
- Be specific about the kind of customer you are looking for.
- Remind the people you are talking to of their role as a center-of-influence to keep them thinking of potential customers.
- Ask them which of the referrals you should contact first.
- Get back to them and let them know you contacted the referrals they gave you.

Lists Selective lists can be prepared that divide the general population by many different characteristics. These lists are prepared by direct marketing associations and are sold to companies for advertising and sales purposes. Some of the lists available include lists organized by streets, age, income, and behavior.

County courthouses also have information on home purchases, business license applications, births, marriages, and deaths. You can also contact the local chapter of the Chamber of Commerce and the Better Business Bureau for prospect lists.

Directories The Yellow Pages are widely used for selective searches. In the Yellow Pages, businesses and organizations are classified by type, making it easy for a salesperson to identify those businesses in a particular industry. For example, if you were selling a new pet food, you could find all local pet stores listed in the Yellow Pages.

Database Marketing In Chapter 2, you learned about database technology. The information stored about current, past, and prospective customers can help direct a company to sell only to qualified customers.

61

REWARDING SALESPEOPLE Online technology is changing the way salespeople are rewarded. Instead of choosing incentive gifts from a catalog or being awarded a particular prize, salespeople can win points during an incentive program. They can use the points through an e-auction program to bid on items available in the program. With a program like this, salespeople are rewarded for top performances and get to enjoy the thrill of bidding on the rewards they love.

THINK CRITICALLY Do you think a salesperson would like this method of rewarding performance? Why or why not?

E-mail Marketing Data is stored about individuals who access a company's Internet site. Many web pages allow prospective customers to e-mail for more information and also provide a telephone number for customers to use to contact the company. Marketing information can be sent to prospective customers via e-mail. The subject headline will determine whether your e-mail is read. Keep it succinct. Because people on the Internet tend to have short attention spans, keep the body of the e-mail short and simple. Give the prospect an incentive to act now and point them in the right direction.

Telequalifying As discussed in Chapter 2, telemarketers can pre-qualify prospective customers and help narrow down the list of contacts to only those individuals who are interested and able to purchase the product or service being sold. By asking the appropriate questions, telemarketers can help the salesperson limit the time spent with contacts who are not the right match for the product or service.

Networking Professional and civic organizations offer many opportunities for a salesperson to meet prospective customers. Networking is the process of finding potential customers through friends, business contacts, coworkers, acquaintances, and fellow members in these organizations. The Internet is also a great networking tool. Many professions have web sites dedicated to networking and sharing of resources.

How are prospective customers found?

3.3 **PROSPECTING FOR SALES**

THE FOUR PROSPECT STYLES

The DISC Inventory, originated in 1928 by Harvard psychologist William Moulton Marston, suggests that most people have four basic behavioral traits or qualities that determine how others perceive them. This has been found to be especially true in workplace behaviors. The traits are as follows.

- Drive
- Influencing ability (also known as interest in people)
- Steadfastness
- Conscientiousness

The DISC theory is based on the premise that each behavioral style is ruled by a different emotional style and that when people are under stress, the negative aspects of their emotional style cause them to act in a way that is annoying or offensive to others. As a salesperson, it will be important for you to control your stress in order to keep customers from disliking you. Knowing your own traits, as well as your prospects' traits, will help you be successful as a salesperson.

By better understanding the behavioral style of your prospects you will

- Have a better understanding of the prospect as a customer
- Be able to establish trust and rapport more easily
- Build better business relationships
- Increase your sales effectiveness

Once you understand why people act the way they do, it will be easier for you to serve your customers and motivate them to purchase products or services from you.

DRIVE

An individual who is classified as a driver is task-oriented, direct, confident, determined, focused on results, competitive, demanding, and controlling. You can identify drivers by their take-charge behavior. They are very outgoing and are always active.

To sell to a driver, you should be direct, concise, and to the point. Engage in small talk with them only if they initiate it. They are more concerned with what you can do for them and when you can do it than with how you are going to do it. Stick to the bottom line with a driver and do not over-explain.

When a driver successfully manages stress, that individual is viewed as pioneering, innovative, forward-looking, and challenge-oriented. Drivers with unmanaged stress come across as demanding, egotistical, aggressive, rude, and undiplomatic.

INFLUENCING ABILITY

An influencing individual is people-oriented, friendly, relaxed, outgoing, emotional, talkative, and expressive. You can identify influencers by their outgoing and active behaviors and their desire to work with others. To successfully sell to influencers, you should socialize, make small talk, spare them the details, and follow up by giving friendly reminders. Show excitement and enthusiasm when meeting with them and let them do the talking.

An influencer who manages stress is seen as optimistic, enthusiastic, and motivational. Such an individual is a team player and a creative problem solver. An influencer with unmanaged stress comes across as inattentive, flighty, and too trusting. This individual is often poor with details and listens only part of the time.

STEADFASTNESS

The steady person is warm, sincere, loyal, stable, predictable, oriented toward cooperation and harmony, supportive, and dependable. The steady person is a good listener and requires a predictable environment. You can identify steady people by their reserved style and their desire to work with others. To successfully sell to steady individuals, you should work to earn their trust, go slow and easy, and give them time to adjust to your proposal. Answer all of their questions and offer reassurance that the purchase is the safe and secure thing for them to do. Always remember to give them time to make adjustments to change.

A steady person with managed stress seems to be stable and sincere, patient and empathetic, logical, and service-oriented. Steady individuals with unmanaged stress come across as too passive, resistant to change, poor with priorities, hesitant, and inflexible.

CONSCIENTIOUSNESS

The conscientious individual is cautious, calculated, analytical, task-oriented, reserved, detail-oriented, and focused on quality. To successfully sell to conscientious prospects, you should be prepared and structured. You should tell them what you will do and how you will do it. Provide evidence in the form of proof and testimonials to support your claims about the product you are selling. If there is a downside to your sales proposal, address it upfront. Do not wait until later in the presentation or allow prospects to find it for themselves.

With managed stress, a conscientious person is seen as being careful and thorough, objective and clear, having high standards, and being a good analyzer. With unmanaged stress, the individual gets lost in the details and appears fussy and critical, picky and pessimistic, and cool and aloof.

Why is knowledge of behavioral qualities important in selling?

_____

_____

3.3 PROSPECTING FOR SALES

THINK CRITICALLY

1. What is the difference between blind and selective searches?
   _____
   _____

2. What are types of blind searches?
   _____
   _____
   _____

3. What are types of selective searches?
   _____
   _____
   _____

4. Name the four behavioral styles defined by the DISC Inventory and list the main characteristics of each style.
   _____
   _____
   _____
   _____
   _____
   _____

5. List someone you know who you think represents each of the behavioral styles discussed. Tell why you think each person fits the specific category.
   _____
   _____
   _____
   _____

MAKE CONNECTIONS

6. **RESEARCH** You are a photographer looking for prospective customers. Look through the local newspaper and make a list of anyone that you read about who might have a need for or be interested in your services. Tell why each person could be a prospective customer for you.

7. **PROBLEM SOLVING** Tell which type of search method—blind or selective—you would use and why you would choose that method to find prospects if you were selling each of the following items: light bulbs, subscriptions to more than 100 different magazines, time shares for a Hawaiian condominium development, a car wax developed especially for car detailing businesses, and home security systems that appeal to owners of luxury homes. Present your answers in an attractive format.

8. **COMMUNICATION** Choose one of the behavioral styles defined by the DISC Inventory. Prepare a presentation about the traits of a person with that style. Include examples of famous people that you think fit the style. Present your presentation to your classmates.

65

REVIEW

CHAPTER SUMMARY

LESSON 3.1 Psychology of Selling

A. Customers buy products based on their needs at the time of the purchase. Needs are arranged from physiological needs to self-actualization needs in Maslow's Hierarchy of Needs. A customer cannot fill upper-level needs until lower-level needs have been met.

B. Relationship selling emphasizes the relationship between a salesperson and a buyer. In relationship selling, salespeople need to learn as much about customers as possible and build a trusting relationship with them.

LESSON 3.2 Knowledge for Selling

A. Salespeople need to have a thorough knowledge of the product being sold when presenting information to a prospective customer.

B. In addition to customer and product knowledge, salespeople should know all about the company they work for and the industry they work in as well as who their market is and who their competition is.

LESSON 3.3 Prospecting for Sales

A. There are many ways to locate prospective customers. Blind searches are a random attempt to find and identify prospects. Selective searches, which are prospecting methods that are not random, usually produce better results than blind searches.

B. The DISC Inventory defines four behavioral types that are exhibited by most individuals in the workplace. If you know the type of behavior prospective customers exhibit, you will be able to work with them more effectively in the sales process.

VOCABULARY BUILDER

Choose the term that best fits the definition. Write the letter of the answer in the space provided. Some terms may not be used.

_____ 1. Direct communication between a salesperson and a prospective customer

_____ 2. Physical characteristics or capabilities of a product

_____ 3. Advantages of a product resulting from its features

_____ 4. Arranges needs in ascending order of importance

_____ 5. Emphasizes the relationship between a salesperson and a buyer

_____ 6. Tells the customer who you are, what you do, and what you can do for him or her

_____ 7. Group of businesses with similar products

_____ 8. Process of searching for potential customers

a. benefits
b. blind search
c. features
d. general benefit strategy
e. industry
f. Maslow's Hierarchy of Needs
g. personal selling
h. prospecting
i. relationship selling
j. selective search

CHAPTER 3

REVIEW CONCEPTS

9. What does the salesperson have to do in the personal selling process?

10. If a prospective customer does not know about the benefits of a product, what will be the likely outcome of the sales process?

11. Using Maslow's theory, explain what motivates buyers.

12. Why is relationship selling replacing the traditional personal selling approach?

13. How can a salesperson learn about a customer?

14. What can a salesperson do to increase the chance of getting a prospective customer's attention?

15. Why should a salesperson have knowledge of the industry, the market, the company, and the competition?

16. What is the purpose of prospecting?

REVIEW

17. What is the purpose of applying selective criteria before doing a prospect search?

_____
_____
_____

18. Why are current customers a good source of referrals?

_____
_____
_____

19. Why is it important to understand the behavioral style of prospects?

_____
_____
_____

20. If you were selling to someone with "drive" behavioral traits, what would be important to remember about his or her typical behavior?

_____
_____
_____

21. If you were selling to someone with "steadfastness" behavioral traits, what would be important to remember about getting along with that customer if he or she was not dealing effectively with stress?

_____
_____
_____

APPLY WHAT YOU LEARNED

22. Describe an experience you have had when personal selling was used. Tell what was effective about the experience and what you did not like.

_____
_____
_____

23. Have you ever shopped somewhere where the salesperson recognized you and remembered things about you? (If you have not, ask an adult to share a relationship selling experience he or she has had.) How did it make you feel about doing business with that salesperson? Would you look for that salesperson if you were going to purchase a similar item in the future?

_____
_____
_____

CHAPTER 3

24. Which type of blind search do you think is used most often? Why do you think companies choose this method?

_____
_____
_____

25. With which types of selective searches are you familiar? What types of companies use them and what products do they sell?

_____
_____
_____

26. Since behavioral traits are affected by stress, what are things you would look for in customers to determine if they are under stress? How could you tell if they were or were not managing their stress effectively?

_____
_____
_____

MAKE CONNECTIONS

27. RESEARCH Search the Internet for information on the sales philosophy of a company. Write a brief summary explaining the company's approach to selling.

28. COMMUNICATION Draw a diagram of Maslow's Hierarchy of Needs by using a graphics software package or by preparing a poster. Label each level of need, and list at least five needs for each level on your diagram. Present this information to your classmates.

29. BUSINESS MATH Use a spreadsheet to calculate the retail price for each of the following items. All answers should be expressed as currency with two decimal places.

Product	Cost	Percent Markup	Retail Price
Men's dress shirt	$28.00	60%	_____
Girl's jeans	$19.50	33.33%	_____
Girl's dress	$74.50	35%	_____
Women's boots	$65.00	75%	_____
Men's boots	$80.00	80%	_____

30. RESEARCH You have been hired as a sales representative for a company that publishes high school yearbooks. Your job is to visit schools, call on the yearbook sponsors, and persuade them to let your company publish their yearbook. These sponsors will have a variety of behavioral styles. In order to prepare yourself for the sales calls, write your strategy for working with each of the behavioral styles described in the DISC Inventory.

CHAPTER 4

DEVELOPING THE SALE

LESSONS

4.1 THE PRE-APPROACH

4.2 MEETING A NEED

4.3 HANDLING OBJECTIONS

CAREERS IN SELLING

CREATIVE MEMORIES

Founded in 1987 in St. Cloud, Minnesota, Creative Memories is a direct-selling organization with more than 50,000 consultants worldwide. Creative Memories offers consumers techniques and supplies for organizing, documenting, and preserving photographs and memorabilia.

Consultants educate and provide hands-on assistance during home classes and workshops. The home class serves as a foundation for a Consultant's business as she or he sells, takes reorders, develops a customer base, and recruits others to join the Creative Memories sales force. In workshops, customers can complete albums and buy additional products.

A Consultant has unlimited earning potential and determines earnings by her or his own personal goals and achievements. Creative Memories provides a step-by-step start-up program and support materials designed for the beginning Consultant. The Success Plan allows new Consultants to earn free products during their first 90 days.

THINK CRITICALLY
1. What are the advantages of operating a home-based business like Creative Memories?
2. What skills other than selling would a Consultant need in order to be successful?

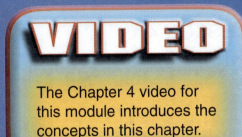

The Chapter 4 video for this module introduces the concepts in this chapter.

PROJECT
Planning the Sale

PROJECT OBJECTIVES
- Develop a pre-approach
- Determine how to help a prospect establish a need
- Anticipate and handle objections

GETTING STARTED
Read through the Project Process below. Make a list of any materials you will need. Decide how you will get the needed materials or information. You are employed by the company that makes your favorite soft drink. Think about each of the following.
- Why do you like this soft drink?
- What do you know about the product and the company?
- Where could you find more product information?
- Who would your competition be in selling this soft drink?

PROJECT PROCESS

Part 1 LESSON 4.1 Using the soft drink you have chosen, develop a sales approach for selling this product. You will be selling the soft drink to restaurants that currently use a rival product. Make a list of at least five prospective customers in your area and develop a script for a lead-qualifying call. Make a list of the features and benefits of the soft drink.

Part 2 LESSON 4.2 Assume you will meet with three of the prospective customers. Summarize what you know about each of the restaurants. If you don't think you know enough about them, use the Internet or other resources to gather more information. Make a list of points you will discuss with the prospects at the beginning of your meeting. What are some questions you can ask? What type of presentation will you use? Will you use the same type of presentation for all three restaurants?

Part 3 LESSON 4.3 Make a list of objections you think customers might have about the soft drink and decide how you will respond to the objections.

CHAPTER REVIEW

Project Wrap-up Using the information you have gathered, develop a presentation that you could use with one of the prospects. If possible, use multimedia software to make the presentation. Give the presentation to your class.

LESSON 4.1
THE PRE-APPROACH

EXPLAIN the importance of lead qualification

DESCRIBE the importance of the first 30 seconds in the pre-approach contact

DESCRIBE the important aspects of closing the call

LEAD QUALIFICATION

As you learned in Chapter 3, telemarketers sometimes handle lead qualification and pass on the names of qualified prospects to the sales force. However, as a salesperson you may be responsible for the **pre-approach**—the initial contact with a prospect. This is often referred to as the "make it" or "break it" step of the sales process. A successful pre-approach gets you in the door for an appointment with a prospect and a potential sale. A poorly-prepared or unsuccessful pre-approach results in a missed opportunity.

WHY QUALIFY LEADS

Lead qualification determines whether or not a prospect has three things—a recognized need, buying power, and receptivity and accessibility. Each of these is important in qualifying leads. All three must be present before a salesperson will want to spend time and energy calling on a prospect.

ON THE $CENE

Being chosen as the organizers for Memorable Machines, their school's annual car show, was exciting for Buz and Carol. Their first task was to sell sponsors on the idea of the car show. In preparing to call on prospective sponsors, they know they need to develop an introductory script to use when making the first call to a company. What information do you think they should include in the script?

4.1 **THE PRE-APPROACH**

A Recognized Need Some prospects are aware that they have an unsatisfied need, but there are other prospects who may realize they have a need only after receiving a little more information from the salesperson about the product or service. Asking the right questions can help a salesperson determine if there is a need. Questions to ask include the following.

- How satisfied are you with your current situation?
- How does this situation affect your productivity, your profits, or your morale?
- How important would it be to eliminate this problem?
- Are you dissatisfied enough to take action today?

Buying Power To avoid wasting time and money, the salesperson needs to identify the individual who has the purchasing authority and be sure the company has the ability to pay before scheduling a presentation. When calling on a business, time spent researching the company's organizational chart and the credit standing helps you find the right person to contact.

Receptivity and Accessibility The prospect must be willing to see the salesperson and must be accessible to the salesperson. Some prospects refuse to see all salespeople. Some with high-ranking positions will see only a salesperson with a similar rank.

Many times you will have to get by *screeners*, individuals who answer calls for the prospects you are trying to contact. You should deal with screeners in a professional manner because they will determine whether or not you get through to the prospect. If someone referred you to the company, be sure to mention the name of that individual early in the call. You will need to tell the screener the purpose of your call, but do not get into the details. Try to ask the screeners questions that they cannot answer. This may persuade them to put you through to the prospects you are trying to reach.

> **did you KNOW?**
>
> You can find information on a company's credit standing by checking its Standard & Poor's rating. This information can be found on the Web or at your local library.

VOICE MAIL

If you reach a prospect's voice mail, do not leave a message the first few times. Try calling at different times of the day to see if the prospect will answer. If after repeated tries you do not reach the prospect, then you should leave a message. Try leaving your name, number, and a convenient time you can be reached. Do not leave any other details about why you are calling. Prospects may be more inclined to call you back if they think you could be a prospective customer of theirs.

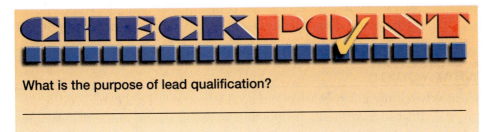

What is the purpose of lead qualification?

CHAPTER 4 DEVELOPING THE SALE

CASHLESS PAYMENTS Imagine going into a fast-food establishment and not having to pay with cash. Cashless payments are the wave of the future and now are being tested in some markets. This technology will help put the "fast" back in fast food. More than ever before, customers are tuned in to technology and automation, and they will be demanding changes such as this in their business transactions. In cashless payment transactions, a company sells a card similar to a debit card to customers. Each time the customer makes a purchase, the card is swiped, and the money spent is subtracted from the balance on the card. From a sales perspective, if customers have a debit card from your company, they will always come back to your business to use it. Another advantage of using debit cards is that counter sales employees will be free from receiving money and making change, which will result in fewer errors.

THINK CRITICALLY What are the advantages and disadvantages of cashless payments to customers?

Write a script for the first 30 seconds of a lead-qualifying call you could use to sell the prospect your special recipe for chocolate chip cookies.

THE FIRST 30 SECONDS

When calling prospects for the pre-approach, the most important rule to remember is to keep it brief. You do not want to get into a long conversation with the prospect at this point. If you talk too much, you may lose the chance to meet with the prospect. And no matter how much you talk, you cannot make the sale over the telephone.

In the first 30 seconds of the conversation, you need to communicate the following.

- Who you are and what company you represent
- What you do
- Why you are calling
- Why the prospect should invest time in meeting with you

WHO YOU ARE AND WHAT COMPANY YOU REPRESENT

At this stage, state your name and the name of your company. You may also want to give a short description of your company. For example, you could say, "Hi, my name is Gloria Mendez from Music Express, a stereo equipment distributor."

WHAT YOU DO

Creatively tell the prospect what you do. Do not say, "I sell compact disc players." Instead, say, "I help people find ways to listen to music the way the recording artist intended for it to be heard."

4.1 THE PRE-APPROACH

WHY YOU ARE CALLING

This is your chance to ask the prospect a question that will make him or her stop and think. When formulating this question, think about the type of information you want to get. Can you qualify the prospect as a result of the question? Will you need to ask additional questions to get the information you need? Will the question make the prospect think? Does the question separate you from your competitors?

Based on the answer your prospect gives, you will be able to respond with appropriate information about the reason for your call.

Successful Openings for Lead-Qualifying Calls

Referral This is usually a powerful door opener. Be clear on the name and organization of the person that made the referral. If you met the person through a professional organization, be sure to name the organization.

Your Track Record Emphasize success stories with other clients and what these cases imply you can do for the prospect.

What You Can Do Briefly outline what you believe you can do for the prospect.

Request Follow-Up If the prospect has requested more information, be sure you make it clear that you are following up on the prospect's earlier request. This may have come from your company's web site or from a promotional activity conducted by your company.

Phrases to Avoid in Lead-Qualifying Calls

How are you this evening?

Is this a good time to talk?

Hold on.

I can't…

But…

I don't know.

The only thing we can do…

WORKSHOP

In a group, brainstorm to create a list of additional phrases to avoid when making lead-qualifying calls.

WHY THE PROSPECT SHOULD INVEST TIME IN MEETING WITH YOU

Instigate a call for action from the prospect. Generate a reason for the prospect to meet with you. For example, tell the prospect that you'd like to demonstrate the features and benefits of your company's newest product.

What is the importance of the first 30 seconds of a lead-qualifying call?

CLOSING THE CALL

If the prospect asks for more information about what you do, speak in terms of overall concepts without getting into technical details. If you provide too much information during the pre-approach call, the prospect may not see a need to meet with you face to face. Emphasize the problem solving that you do and your end results.

Be ready to suggest a time for the prospect to meet with you. If you schedule meetings with more than one prospect, try to group your meetings in the same geographic region in order to save travel time. Give the prospect a range of choices by asking questions like, "Are mornings or afternoons better for you?"

Once you have an appointment, get off the telephone as quickly as you can. Be sure the prospect has your phone number in the event something unexpected should come up. Do not waste the prospect's time by asking for directions to the prospect's location. Use an Internet map site or ask to be connected to an administrative assistant or receptionist for assistance. Be sure to write down notes regarding your conversation as soon as you end the phone call. You will want to revisit your notes prior to your sales meeting and be prepared to address any questions or objections raised by the prospect during the course of the phone call.

CHECKPOINT

When closing the call, why is it best to provide only general concepts rather than technical details?

4.1 THE PRE-APPROACH

THINK CRITICALLY

1. Why do you think the pre-approach is referred to as the "make it" or "break it" step of the sales process?

   ___

2. Describe the three things that must be present in order to qualify a lead.

   ___

3. Why is it important in the first 30 seconds of a lead-qualifying call to introduce yourself and your company and explain what you do, why you are calling, and why the prospect should meet with you?

   ___

4. Why do you think "Is this a good time to talk?" is not a good opener for a lead-qualifying call?

   ___

5. What are the advantages to you in being the one who suggests the time for a meeting with a prospect?

   ___

MAKE CONNECTIONS

6. **RESEARCH** Use the Internet to research directory listings available online. Make a list of web sites you could use for telephone number information if you were going to do a blind search for prospective customers.

7. **COMMUNICATION** Make a tape recording of yourself role playing a 30-second lead-qualifying call. Listen to the recording and evaluate yourself on professional sound, enthusiasm, knowledge of product and market, and quality and tempo of voice. Write a summary of your evaluation.

8. **PROBLEM SOLVING** You are selling timeshares at a new resort on a Florida beach. You are calling numbers at random from a directory arranged by address. All you know about the prospects is that they live in an upper-middle-class neighborhood in Birmingham, Alabama. Compose some possible questions you could use in a lead-qualifying call to find out more information.

CHAPTER 4 DEVELOPING THE SALE

LESSON 4.2
MEETING A NEED

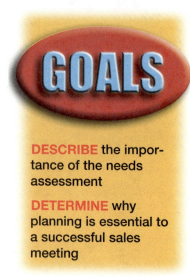

GOALS

DESCRIBE the importance of the needs assessment

DETERMINE why planning is essential to a successful sales meeting

NEEDS ASSESSMENT

One of the goals of a salesperson is to find out as much as possible about the prospect's situation. This is done through a **needs assessment** that involves interviewing the customer to determine his or her specific needs and wants and the range of options the customer has for satisfying them.

ESTABLISHING THE NEED

The heart of the interview phase of the sales process involves establishing and solving the problem. If this part is not successfully completed, the prospect will not realize the need for your product or service. Since the handling of objections is important to accomplish a sale, a successful salesperson will anticipate the objections prospects might have and will include information in response to these objections in the presentation.

ON THE $CENE

After contacting prospective sponsors and scheduling appointments to meet with them, Buz and Carol know they have to organize information for the presentations. Since they will be meeting with car dealers, restaurants, automotive supply stores, car detailers, and other retail merchants, they know they will have to develop several different presentations because each of the businesses will have different reasons for being a car show sponsor. Do you think Buz and Carol are right to match the presentations to the interests of the different businesses?

4.2 MEETING A NEED

When prospects know what they want, fulfilling their needs is referred to as *need satisfying*. Even in need satisfying situations, the salesperson must be flexible and willing to commit company resources and selling time in order to better satisfy needs. When the need is not identified, the process of satisfying the need is called *problem resolution*. Problem resolution requires the salesperson to adopt the prospect's point of view, ask questions to assess the nature of needs and requirements, and act as a consultant to assist the prospect in solving the problem.

INTERVIEWING TECHNIQUES

As you learned in Chapter 3, customer knowledge is important in relationship selling. You will need to expand your knowledge of prospective customers when you meet with them for the first time. Remember that open-ended questions will get more information from prospects. Some things you should be sure to ask about include the following.

- **The Person** These questions make customers feel important and give them the opportunity to talk.

- **The Organization** These questions provide insight into the company, its structure, the decision-making process, and the products currently being used.

- **Goals and Obstacles** When you can help a customer meet goals and eliminate objections, you become a valuable resource for them.

PROBING FOR INFORMATION

Probing is an attempt by the salesperson to gain additional sales-related information from the prospect. When the prospect has not volunteered all of the needed information, the salesperson must probe for the information needed. Certain probing techniques can be of special value to the salesperson. The silence probe, the encouragement probe, and the elaboration probe all are seen as neutral probes because the salesperson is not directly asking the prospect for information. The clarification probe and the topic-change probe are not neutral probes because they involve directed informational requests.

Silence Probe When using the *silence probe*, the salesperson refrains from taking the lead in the conversation. The prospect takes the initiative and continues to give needed information. This probe can be useful as long as the prospect reacts. The silence probe does not bias the prospect's thinking. It does slow down the pace of the interview, but it sets the stage for both parties to become more thoughtful.

Encouragement Probe The *encouragement probe* involves behavior on the part of the salesperson that encourages the prospect to continue revealing information. A salesperson might nod or use a similar gesture that will encourage prospects to continue talking. The prospect gets the message from the salesperson that what they are saying is interesting and understood. This probe also slows the pace of the interview, but it is less awkward for the prospect because the salesperson is contributing encouragement.

Elaboration Probe The *elaboration probe* extends the encouragement probe by adding a positive request for more information about a topic that the prospect has already mentioned. Prospects might get so carried away by the salesperson's interest and encouragement in a neutral probe that they start making up product requirements. The salesperson must decide when free talking by the prospect has run its course of usefulness.

Clarification Probe The *clarification probe* includes any questions that request information on a specific subject or situation. It may involve clarification of something volunteered from the neutral probes or something as yet unmentioned. Too often the salesperson is unable to process all the information gathered and convey how he or she can help the prospect. This may be because the salesperson fails to ask the right questions to determine what is truly valuable to the prospect. So the clarification probe can be very helpful. The clarification probe is not considered neutral because it involves directed informational requests.

Topic-Change Probe The *topic-change probe* involves a judgment by the salesperson as to the proper time to stop probing on one topic and either switch to a new topic or make a transition to the next aspect of the interview.

DEVELOPING AND PROPOSING SOLUTIONS

After gathering appropriate information about the needs and wants of the prospect, the next step is to maximize the fit between what you can offer and what the prospect wants and needs. It is time to get the prospect enthused about filling that need with your product or service. This is done in the form of a sales proposal or a presentation. As you learned in Chapter 1, a sales proposal is used to offer a product or service to a client in a written format, and a sales presentation occurs when the salesperson explains how a product or service will benefit the customer. The quality of the sales proposal and the sales presentation is important. The sales presentation might be your only chance to meet with a prospective customer. You must be able to present your proposal and handle any objections confidently and professionally. You will learn more about handling objections in Lesson 4.3.

Why is the needs assessment important to the sales process?

4.2 MEETING A NEED

MAKING THE PITCH

It is essential that you plan your sales presentation carefully in order to communicate effectively the features and benefits of the product or service you are selling. You must also practice the presentation so that you become very familiar with information to be communicated to the prospect.

Some of the benefits of a well-planned presentation include

- Helping you stay on a track that leads to a close and avoids customer objections
- Allowing you to concentrate on the prospect's thoughts and reactions rather than on what you are going to say next
- Keeping you from missing the points that may be pertinent to your prospect's situation
- Helping you gain confidence in your presentations as a selling tool that will bring results
- Enabling prospects to gain more confidence in you

PREPARATION

As you prepare to meet with the prospect, you will have to decide the best way to present the features and benefits of your product or service. The type of presentation you use will depend on the motives of your prospective customers. There are three types of presentations: canned, key-point, and customized. In relationship selling, variations and combinations of all three types are used. As you learned in Chapter 2, it is easy to prepare a multimedia presentation using technology tools. You can make any of these three presentation types by using multimedia technology.

Canned Presentation A **canned presentation** is directed at satisfying the needs of the majority of the customers who could use the product or service. A company will have some salespeople who are more successful than others. By taking the approaches they use and formulating them into a package that can be memorized, these salespeople have developed a canned presentation that can be used on a standardized basis throughout the company. The canned presentation is used more often in door-to-door and telephone sales.

Key-Point Presentation The **key-point presentation** lists major points of the product or service and gives all the reasons for purchasing it. It is arranged in an order that will build customer interest as each point is introduced. The presentation is developed from an outline. The outline often may be the framework for an illustrated presentation brochure. The salesperson can discuss the points in the pre-determined order or as they are brought up by the customer. This key-point presentation is used when the product is complex or when specific features satisfy different customer needs.

Customized Presentation Customers today want creative, customized solutions. The **customized presentation** is based on the specific needs and requirements of the prospect. Information gathered in the preapproach can be used to create a customer profile, which is valuable when developing and using customized presentations.

In a group, brainstorm to generate a list of products and services. Then decide which type of presentation would be the best to use for each product or service. Give reasons for your choices.

BUSINESS MATH CONNECTION

The breakeven point is the point at which sales revenue equals the total cost of producing and distributing a product or service. At the breakeven point, a business has no profit and no loss—it simply breaks even. A business can use the breakeven point in units to analyze whether it is charging an appropriate price for one of its products or services. To calculate the breakeven point in units, a business must determine the selling price, fixed costs, and variable costs for one item or one unit of service. Then, divide the total fixed costs by the selling price minus the variable costs.

If A-1 Stereo Repair has fixed costs of $10,000, charges $75 for each service call, and has $20 in variable costs for each call, what would be the minimum number of service calls it would need to make in one year in order to break even?

SOLUTION

Breakeven point = Total fixed costs ÷ (Selling price − Variable costs)

Breakeven point = $10,000 ÷ ($75 − $20)

Breakeven point = $10,000 ÷ $55 = 181.82

The breakeven point in units would be 182 service calls (rounded up).

THE MEETING

Before going to the prospect's office, make a call to confirm your appointment so that you can be sure the prospect is going to be available. This also lets the prospect know you, too, value your time. If you require any special equipment for your presentation, such as audio visual equipment, be sure to make arrangements ahead of time. You don't want to give anyone the impression that you are unprepared. When you arrive at the prospect's office, give the receptionist your business card and state whom you are there to see. If you see any materials about the company in the waiting area, review them. You may pick up some last minute information for your presentation.

Office environments and furnishings can give you an idea of points to emphasize in your presentation. Modern, up-to-date surroundings and equipment would suggest that you use terms indicating that your product is the newest model available or a step ahead of the rest. Older surroundings and furnishings would be your key to emphasize economy or the cost-savings features of your product.

Meeting the Prospect Introduce yourself and present a business card when meeting the prospect for the first time. Do not provide any other printed materials at this time, or the prospect may read them while you are talking rather than focusing on your presentation. Briefly remind the prospect why you are there. Then take your lead from the prospect. Remember the different personality styles you learned of in Chapter 3 (driving, influencing, steadfastness, and conscientiousness) and try to work with the prospect in the most effective way.

4.2 **MEETING A NEED**

IMPORTANCE OF BODY LANGUAGE

Body language, or nonverbal communication, plays an important role in the sales presentation. Body language includes posture, facial expressions, gestures, and mannerisms. Some studies have shown that nonverbal communication has a bigger impact on others than does verbal communication. The moment you meet with prospects they judge you by what they see and feel.

During a presentation you will need not only to focus on your body language but also the body language of the prospect. You should not only listen carefully to what prospects say but also watch how they are saying it. Body language can tell you a lot about what a prospect is thinking. It is important for you to maintain good eye contact with people when you are presenting. This will help them stay focused on you. By being aware of the prospect's body language, you can sense when something you've said turns away the prospect. When this occurs, you should try using a different selling approach.

Some of the body language clues you should look for include

- **Firm Handshake** Conveys confidence and professionalism.
- **Unbuttoned Suit Jacket** Signals an open attitude and a willingness to talk.
- **Hands Open and Relaxed, Palms Turned Upward** Signals an open, sincere individual who is ready to cooperate.
- **No Eye Contact** Indicates that the individual doesn't like you or something you have said or is not interested in what you are saying.
- **Moves Closer To the Table and Places Elbows on the Table** Shows trust is increasing.
- **Faces and Looks Intently at You with Head Slightly Tilted** Signals that the prospect is interested and is giving careful consideration to your proposal.

CHECKPOINT ✓

What should you do to prepare for a sales presentation?

_____

_____

THINK CRITICALLY

1. Why is establishment of need essential to the sales process?

2. What are three things you should talk about when interviewing a prospect?

3. List and explain the types of probes that are used to get more information from a prospect.

4. Why is a well-planned presentation important?

5. List and describe three types of presentation formats.

MAKE CONNECTIONS

6. **COMMUNICATION** Research body language used in another country. With a partner, role play a selling situation and illustrate appropriate body language for the country you researched.

7. **PROBLEM SOLVING** You are preparing to call on the general manager of a chain of retail clothing stores in your area that has teenagers as its target market. You are selling a new line of customized t-shirts that are designed to appeal to teenagers. Using word processing software, prepare a list of questions you would use in the needs assessment.

8. **BUSINESS MATH** Use a spreadsheet to calculate the breakeven point in units for the following items.

Item	Fixed costs per year	Selling price per unit	Variable costs per unit	Breakeven point per unit
Calculator	$1,800	$69.00	$49.00	
Desk organizer	$3,500	$48.00	$20.00	
Monitor stand	$3,500	$39.00	$19.00	

LESSON 4.3
HANDLING OBJECTIONS

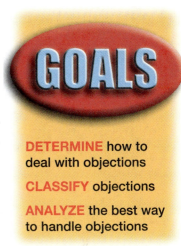

GOALS

DETERMINE how to deal with objections

CLASSIFY objections

ANALYZE the best way to handle objections

DEALING WITH OBJECTIONS

During the sales process, any type of sales resistance by the prospect is an **objection**. Objections can be active or passive, expressed or implied. An objection can be a question with a negative viewpoint, a disagreeing statement, or an outburst of some type. It can be silence or stillness when words or action are sought or an expression or movement denoting disapproval. Salespeople must recognize and accept objections and look at them as ways to uncover concerns, benefits, and buying motives that can help make the sale.

ON THE $CENE

Buz and Carol had several appointments that went very smoothly and, thus far, had secured all of the businesses as sponsors for Memorable Machines. However, when they called on Joe's Mobile Detailing Service, everything changed. Joe did not understand why his assistant had agreed that he would meet with them. He did not see why they thought he would want to be a sponsor, and he did not understand why a school would be having a car show. Buz and Carol tried to explain the concept to him, but he would not listen. They never had a chance to get started with their presentation. Buz and Carol became angry with Joe and were upset when they left. Do you think this was the best way for Buz and Carol to handle Joe's objections?

Zig Ziglar, a well-known sales trainer and motivator, believes that the best time to answer the objection is before it occurs. He goes on to say that if you are consistently getting the same objections after your presentation, it is a sign your presentation is in trouble. In other words, you should prepare carefully for your presentation and try to anticipate any objections the customer might have so that you can address them before the customer has a chance to make them and respond appropriately to any objections that do arise.

RECOGNIZING WHEN OBJECTIONS OCCUR

Objections may occur at any phase of the sales process, so the salesperson must be prepared to handle objections before the interview phase begins. Many times the prospect will voice some type of objection before scheduling an interview with the salesperson. During the interview phase, prospects might object to being told that they have a problem, that the solution offered is satisfactory, or that now is the time to buy.

At any point in the interview phase, the prospect is in one of three states in reference to buying—learning, agreeing, or disagreeing. At each stage of the sales process, the prospect can be receptive to the point of learning, agreeing, or disagreeing. From your perspective as a salesperson, learning and agreeing are the most preferred states of mind for the prospect. However, since disagreeing sometimes will occur, you must be aware that this is a normal response, and you must be prepared to deal with it.

Whether or not the objection is active or passive, expressed or implied, prospect resistance must be met by skillful, effective selling techniques. Salespeople encounter sales resistance that stands in the way of successful selling every day. You must prepare to overcome it.

Many times objections to the purchase are a way of getting rid of the salesperson without buying or a way of avoiding an obligation to buy. Therefore, an objection does not mean that prospects do not need or require your product or service. In most cases, prospects object because they lack information about your products or services. In some cases, prospects may be unaware that they have a need that the product or service you are offering can satisfy. The prospect may also need help in justifying the purchase and in feeling comfortable that making the purchase is the right thing to do.

THE DISAGREEING PROSPECT

Creative selling often involves making a prospect dissatisfied with his or her present situation and then showing the prospect how your product or service

can take away that dissatisfaction. A perfect sales performance would involve moving the prospect through the interview phase of the sales process, generating only positive responses, to the point that the prospect would decide to buy without any hesitation or stress. However, this will rarely, if ever, happen, so as a salesperson you must expect some hesitation and some level of disagreement. If nothing else, objections will occur because customers will have clarification questions.

The prospect's emotional needs, as defined by Maslow's Hierarchy, will be involved in objections. Social acceptance or economic security may affect the prospect's objections. The prospect

4.3 **HANDLING OBJECTIONS**

may not realize what is causing the objections but will be aware of them. You must recognize and handle such objections effectively or risk losing a sale.

SALESPERSON'S ATTITUDE TOWARD OBJECTIONS

Objections can be viewed as shortcuts to sales because they help uncover customer needs and desires. They are the prospect's way of telling the salesperson how to make the sale. Objections help guide the salesperson through the presentation by providing feedback from the prospect indicating which direction to take from a given point. Objections also provide a way for prospects to ask questions without showing how interested they are. In your mind you should turn their objections into questions, and then answer the questions. As a salesperson giving a presentation, you should look at objections that you are unable to prevent as a flaw in the presentation and use your response to the objection as another chance to make the sales presentation a success.

Why does a salesperson need to be ready for objections?
___
___

CLASSIFYING OBJECTIONS

Upon hearing an objection, a salesperson must classify it. This will help determine how to handle the objection. To help you classify the objection, ask yourself the following.

- Does it mean the person is not really a prospect?
- Is it valid?
- Is it the real objection or is it a stall?
- Which phase of the sales process does it involve?

DOES IT MEAN THE PERSON IS NOT REALLY A PROSPECT?

If the individual does not qualify as a prospect, the professional salesperson may not want to attempt the sale. It is either unethical or impossible to sell to someone who has the following characteristics.

- Does not need the product or service
- Is not able to pay for it
- Is not eligible to buy it
- Is committed by contract to buy from someone else

- Does not have the authority to make the buying decision
- Has a strong bias that would prevent him or her from buying from the salesperson

If the objection indicates that the individual does not qualify on one or more of these requirements, the salesperson must determine if the objection is valid or not. If it is, the interview probably should be terminated.

IS IT VALID?

An objection is either valid or invalid. If it is valid, it will count against the decision to purchase the product or service. If it is not valid, you have the opportunity to strengthen your position by offering clarification or by disproving the objection. Prospects may make an invalid objection because of a misunderstanding or because they are trying to avoid revealing the real objection. Either way, valid objections must be overcome, and invalid objections must be disproved and corrected.

IS IT THE REAL OBJECTION OR IS IT A STALL?

The stated objection might not be the real objection because the prospect may be unwilling to reveal the real one. In this case, you should assume that the objection is a stall and proceed to probe for the real reason. Once you find the real objection, you can work to overcome it.

WHICH PHASE OF THE SALES PROCESS DOES IT INVOLVE?

Regardless of the phase of the sales process involved, effective salespeople can get to true objections and overcome them. Effectively overcoming objections requires that a salesperson have product knowledge, sales knowledge, customer knowledge, self-confidence, advance preparation, and the ability to effectively utilize sales tools. It often is helpful to consider objections according to the phase of the sales process they involve.

Gaining the Interview Resistance to granting an interview usually surfaces with statements like "I'm too busy," "See me later," or "We've already made a purchase." These examples are likely to be stalls used to cover up real reasons. If you correctly perceive that the objection simply reflects resistance to granting an interview, you can handle it more satisfactorily.

Establishing the Problem When the prospect tells you that another product is taking care of whatever need you identify, this is your key that the prospect does not feel that a problem exists. It is critical to handle objections at this phase of the sale immediately.

Solving the Problem If prospects tell you that they are satisfied with their current supplier, it can indicate an objection to granting you an interview or an objection to your product as the best solution to their problem. Be sure that you and the prospects have agreed on each step as you move through the sales process. If you have done this, you will know whether they are objecting to the interview or the product.

Closing the Sale Since the final decision on whether or not to buy immediately is one that is binding, there is more reason for resistance to occur at this phase. Remember to determine if the objection is valid and handle it accordingly.

4.3 HANDLING OBJECTIONS

CHECKPOINT ✓

What is the importance of classifying objections?

_____

_____

RULES FOR HANDLING OBJECTIONS

Salespeople must handle objections carefully, and overcome them if they want to make a sale. There are four general rules to help improve the salesperson's ability to handle objections. Although these rules may seem obvious, they are often overlooked in the sales process.

- Show interest and understanding
- Listen
- Do not interrupt
- Restate the objection

SHOW INTEREST AND UNDERSTANDING

Showing interest and understanding when the prospect is talking indicates both good manners and good sense. In fact, the salesperson must adopt the customer's point of view. Visualizing what the customer will gain provides a path to customer satisfaction and successful selling. However, the salesperson who does not have a positive attitude toward objections and an understanding of the psychology of the resisting prospect often lets impatience, irritation, and even disgust show. The prospect's awareness of such negative factors can result in a lost sale.

WORKSHOP

In a group, discuss sales transactions you have been involved in when the salesperson broke one of these rules and tell how it made you feel.

GETTING OFF TO A GLOBAL START

The International Trade Administration, part of the United States Department of Commerce, has Foreign Commercial Service Programs available at a low cost. These programs will help you learn how business is conducted in a market you are thinking of entering so that you can do business in the same manner. You will also learn to stay focused on the objective you have for the market and what you hope to accomplish.

THINK CRITICALLY Why do you think a salesperson would need to know this kind of information?

LISTEN

As you learned in Chapter 1, listening is a necessary element of communication. This is true for the salesperson who is encountering sales resistance. Listening requires concentration. You cannot think ahead to your reply while the prospect is talking. If you do not listen, you may miss important information and end up with an unhappy prospect. You might also give the wrong answer to an objection or answer the wrong objection. You must be a good listener, be sensitive to the needs of others, and serve as an adviser to the prospect.

DO NOT INTERRUPT

No one likes to be interrupted when talking. This is especially true in a sales situation. The prospect always must be heard. This will help you make the sale. Some of the reasons that salespeople interrupt prospects when they are making objections are listed below.

- Lack of awareness of the consequences.

- Carrying over the habit from other, more casual conversations.

- Eagerness to answer the objection. The salesperson may anticipate what he thinks the objection is going to be and may want to show how well prepared he is. However, the anticipation of the objection may not be correct.

- A feeling that if the prospect puts the objection into words it will be harder to handle. Usually, this is not true. If the salesperson is patient, the prospect often will voice an objection, see that it is not valid, and discard it.

The salesperson must avoid interrupting the prospect. If the prospect has the opportunity to voice objections, it can help the salesperson find the true nature of the objection and how to approach it.

RESTATE THE OBJECTION

There are three good reasons for restating an objection before answering it. First, the prospect may be pleased to hear the objection quoted. It is a compliment to give another person's ideas emphasis by restating them and an insult to ignore them and give no feedback.

Second, the salesperson may have misunderstood the objection. This could be due to lack of listening skills on the part of the salesperson or the fact that ideas often are not put into words as intended.

Third, the impact of the objection, as stated by the prospect, can be reduced by the salesperson expressing the same idea in other words. This will protect the prospect's ego as well as give the salesperson an opportunity to take another chance to emphasize product features and benefits.

CHECKPOINT

Why is it important for you to handle objections carefully?

_____

_____

4.3 HANDLING OBJECTIONS

THINK CRITICALLY

1. When should a salesperson think about objections?
   _____
   _____
   _____

2. What causes prospects to have objections?
   _____
   _____
   _____

3. What attitude should salespeople have when answering objections?
   _____
   _____
   _____

4. Why is the phase of the sales process where the objection occurs important to the salesperson?
   _____
   _____
   _____

5. Summarize the rules for handling objections.
   _____
   _____

MAKE CONNECTIONS

6. **RESEARCH** You have just been hired as a sales representative for a company that specializes in digital cameras. Make a list of the objections you think you will hear from customers during the pre-approach. Research information on digital cameras and find things that you could say to customers to help ease their objections.

7. **PROBLEM SOLVING** Read each of the statements below. With a partner, discuss whether you think the objection is valid or invalid. Give reasons for your responses.

   A. I'll think it over.
   B. I don't like that color.
   C. This doesn't seem heavy enough.
   D. That's not for me.
   E. Your repair service is too slow.

8. **COMMUNICATION** With a partner, role play for your class a sales situation where the rules for handling objections are handled correctly. Then repeat the role play and break all the rules. Discuss with your classmates the difference in the two scenarios and the effect each would have on the customer.

REVIEW

CHAPTER SUMMARY

LESSON 4.1 The Pre-Approach
A. The pre-approach is considered to be the "make it" or "break it" step of the sales process. Lead qualification is important because a prospect must have a recognized need, buying power, and receptivity and accessibility.
B. The first 30 seconds of the pre-approach is your chance to sell yourself and your ability to help the prospect. If you cannot convince the prospect to meet with you, there will not be an opportunity for a sale.
C. When closing the call, speak in overall concepts and do not provide lots of details. Set up an appointment and then end the call quickly.

LESSON 4.2 Meeting a Need
A. Needs assessments are conducted by interviewing the prospect and probing for information. Once a need is determined, you are ready to offer a solution.
B. A well-planned presentation is essential to the sales process. You should plan and rehearse the presentation several times so that you can concentrate on the prospect's reaction and body language during the sales pitch.

LESSON 4.3 Handling Objections
A. Objections are any type of sales resistance by the prospect. To be successful, a salesperson must be tuned in to the product and the prospect and try to answer all objections before they occur.
B. When an objection occurs, the salesperson should decide what it means. It may or may not be a valid objection. Based on the phase of the sales process you are in, an objection can mean different things.
C. When an objection is made, a salesperson should show interest and understanding, listen carefully, not interrupt the prospect, and restate the objection.

VOCABULARY BUILDER

Choose the term that best fits the definition. Write the letter of the answer in the space provided. Some terms may not be used.

_____ 1. The initial contact with a prospect

_____ 2. Determines whether or not a prospect has a recognized need, buying power, and receptivity and accessibility

_____ 3. Any type of sales resistance by the prospect

_____ 4. An attempt by the salesperson to gain additional sales-related information from the prospect

_____ 5. Directed at satisfying the needs of the majority of the customers who could use the product

_____ 6. Interviewing a customer to determine his or her specific needs and wants and the range of options for satisfying them

a. canned presentation
b. customized presentation
c. key-point presentation
d. lead qualification
e. needs assessment
f. objection
g. pre-approach
h. probing

CHAPTER 4

REVIEW CONCEPTS

7. What is the purpose of the pre-approach?

8. Explain the importance of treating a call screener professionally.

9. What should you do if you reach a prospect's voice mail?

10. When telling a prospective customer the reason for your call, what approach should you use?

11. How do you close a call with a prospective customer?

12. What is the difference between need satisfying and problem resolution?

13. When does a salesperson need to probe?

14. Why must a salesperson be aware of body language?

15. Why is it important for the salesperson to anticipate customer objections?

POINT YOUR BROWSER

b2000.swep.com

REVIEW

16. What would make a salesperson decide a prospective customer is not really a prospect?
_____
_____
_____

17. What is the difference between a valid and an invalid objection?
_____
_____

18. When might a prospect use a stall?
_____
_____

19. When establishing need during the selling process, what problem do you face if a customer tells you the company's current product meets its needs just fine?
_____
_____

20. One of the rules for handling objections is to restate the objection. Why is restating the objection to the prospect a good way to handle an objection?
_____
_____
_____

APPLY WHAT YOU LEARNED

21. Describe how a salesperson can help prospects recognize a need they do not realize they have.
_____
_____
_____
_____

22. Give examples of sales situations when you would use the following probes.

Silence probe _____

Encouragement probe _____

Clarification probe _____

Topic-change probe _____

23. Read the following objections and select the best response and the worst response that a salesperson could make to the customer.

   A. I don't think I care for the color.

   (1) But it is a nice neutral color.
   (2) What color did you have in mind?
   (3) This color has been very popular.
   (4) You will learn to like the color.

   Best response _____ Worst response _____

   B. It's too big for the room.

   (1) I think we can order it in a smaller size.
   (2) Couldn't it fit in another room?
   (3) Not really.
   (4) What size is your room?

   Best response _____ Worst response _____

   C. It will be hard to keep clean.

   (1) It's machine washable.
   (2) You will only want to wear it for dress-up occasions.
   (3) Don't worry about it. There's a special cleaner you can buy.
   (4) The cleaning instructions are on the tag.

   Best response _____ Worst response _____

   D. I have always bought another brand.

   (1) I understand that brand isn't as good as it used to be.
   (2) Then you may want to consider a change.
   (3) Yes, that is a good brand, but this one is recognized as an excellent product.
   (4) The brand of the product isn't important.

   Best response _____ Worst response _____

MAKE CONNECTIONS

24. **RESEARCH** Search the Internet for information on body language in the United States and other countries. Prepare a chart showing how the meaning of gestures varies from country to country.

25. **COMMUNICATION** Develop a canned presentation that could be used at orientation for new students at your school to sell spirit shirts and other logo items. Make this sales presentation for your classmates.

26. **COMMUNICATION** A written sales proposal often is sent to prospects before you meet with them in person. You work for a video production company and have been asked to submit a proposal for a video promoting business classes for the National Business Education Association. Prepare the cover sheet and cover letter for the proposal. The letter should be addressed to Ms. Noelle Sotack, National Business Education Association, 123 Anywhere Street, Washington, DC 20002.

CHAPTER 5

CLOSING AND BEYOND

LESSONS

5.1 CLOSING AND THE SALES PROCESS

5.2 METHODS OF CLOSING

5.3 AFTER THE SALE

CAREERS IN SELLING

DELTA AIRLINES

For more than 70 years, Delta Airlines, Inc., has been a world leader in air transportation for passengers and freight. Delta serves 201 cities in 45 states, the District of Columbia, Puerto Rico, and the U.S. Virgin Islands, as well as 50 cities in 32 other countries.

Delta provides its employees with a variety of career and development opportunities as well as an excellent total compensation and benefits package, which includes paid training and travel privileges. Delta continually seeks skilled, energetic, professional individuals who are committed to providing superior customer service.

One entry-level position is Reservation Sales and Service Representative. This person handles incoming passenger telephone calls and books reservations while serving the customer in an efficient, courteous, and accurate manner. Applicants must be at least 18 years of age, have a high school diploma or equivalency, and be able to type at least 20 words per minute. The position requires excellent telephone and communication skills.

THINK CRITICALLY
1. What would be some of the benefits of working for Delta?
2. What skills could you develop to help you qualify for this position?

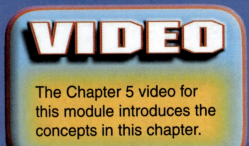

The Chapter 5 video for this module introduces the concepts in this chapter.

PROJECT
Closing the Sale

PROJECT OBJECTIVES
- Prepare for closing
- Explore closing methods and select a method to use for selling a product
- Develop a customer follow-up plan

GETTING STARTED
Read through the Project Process below. Make a list of any materials you will need. Decide how you will get the needed materials or information.
- What products would you most like to sell?
- How would you go about finding prospective customers?
- What are the steps in the sales process you would follow?

PROJECT PROCESS

Part 1 LESSON 5.1 Using the product you have chosen, develop a sales process, from the needs assessment interview to the closing and follow-up.
- Who are your prospects and how will you find them?
- What do you know about the features and benefits of the product and the competition for sales?
- What approach will you use to sell the product?
- Are there any laws that apply to the sale of this product?

Part 2 LESSON 5.2 Continue developing the sales process.
- Which closing method will you use?
- Why did you choose this method over others?
- What will you do if the prospect says "no"? How will you know when it is time to give up?

Part 3 LESSON 5.3 Develop a follow-up plan. Describe the follow-up activities you will conduct with your customers and tell why you chose them.

CHAPTER REVIEW

Project Wrap-up Working with a partner, role play the sales process you have described. Acting as the prospect, your partner should exhibit behaviors for a prospect who is ready to close and should also express some objections. As the salesperson, you should handle the objections appropriately.

CHAPTER 5 CLOSING AND BEYOND

LESSON 5.1
CLOSING AND THE SALES PROCESS

EXPLAIN how a salesperson knows when it is time to close

IDENTIFY legal considerations that affect the sales process

APPROACHING THE CLOSE

The goal of every sales presentation is to close the sale. **Closing** means the customer accepts the product or service you are selling and purchases it. In a well-planned presentation, the closing will be a natural part of the sale. It should not involve tricking the customer or putting pressure on the customer to buy. Throughout the sales process, you work with customers to establish needs in their minds and offer solutions to their problems. The closing process leads the customer to a wise buying decision. The close begins at the start of the presentation by building agreement and helping the prospect decide *how* to buy. By using proper questioning techniques, you can help the prospect complete the transaction and lead the customer to closing. Closing is the final step in the sales process.

ON THE $CENE

Runjan had worked in sales for an office equipment supplier for almost two months. He was very excited when he was hired, but as he went on sales calls, he discovered that he was frightened when it was time to ask the prospect for an order. He was afraid that the prospect would tell him "No!" Runjan's manager was concerned about his low sales performance. She felt that Runjan had the skills, knowledge, and personality to be successful in sales. She called Runjan into the office to talk with him about his problems. What advice do you think the manager should give Runjan?

5.1 CLOSING AND THE SALES PROCESS

Closing cannot take place unless there has been an interview, a problem has been established, and the problem has been solved. During these steps of the sales process, you present sales information, demonstrate the product, eliminate resistance, and bring the prospect to the point of agreeing to the purchase.

PSYCHOLOGY OF CLOSING

A salesperson can make an outstanding presentation and still leave without a deal. This usually happens because the salesperson is not comfortable asking for the sale. Some salespeople may fear that the prospect will see them as pushy or overly assertive. But if the salesperson does not ask for the sale, it may never occur.

Overcoming Closing Fears The prospect expects to be asked for an order. If you do not ask for the order, the prospect's time has been wasted. The salesperson must be prepared to close the sale before actually attempting the close. The following tips will help you overcome any closing fears you may have.

- Be sure the sales process has been properly developed. A need must be established, and questions must be answered. The prospect should understand all of the features and benefits of the product.

- Be well prepared and informed so that you can deal with any last-minute questions and concerns the prospect may have.

- Have an objective for each sales call. If the goal is to establish needs, that is where you should focus your efforts. If the goal is to solve the problem, focus on that. If your goal is closing, then close. Staying focused on your goal will keep you from pushing the process along too quickly.

WHY SALES DO NOT CLOSE

Poor closing techniques are most often blamed when a sale does not close. However, most lost sales can be traced to problems in the development of the sales process.

Lack of Interest The prospect may have come into the interview process unwillingly and may resent the interruption of time the sales presentation is creating. To overcome this problem, you must raise the prospect's interest level and help the prospect establish need.

Lost Awareness During the sales process, the prospect may lose awareness of the problem the salesperson is attempting to solve. Until awareness of the problem is reestablished, the sale cannot be made.

99

Not Convinced The prospect may not be ready to close when the salesperson attempts to close because the prospect may not yet be sure the product is the best solution to his or her problem. The salesperson needs to spend more time solving the prospect's problem before attempting to close.

Other Concerns Even though the prospect allowed the salesperson to make the presentation, there may be a concern about the salesperson or the company. This might be a concern the prospect will not share with the salesperson, and the prospect might use another excuse for not closing the sale.

WHEN TO CLOSE

Once you have established the needs of the prospect, offered a solution to the needs, and answered any objections or concerns, it is time to close the sale. Reaching this point may take several meetings with the prospect or it may come within a few minutes of your initial meeting. It will depend on the prospect, the product or service being sold, and the salesperson. There is no one best time to close the sale. The salesperson must be alert to feedback received from the prospect to know when to attempt to close.

Expression An experienced salesperson might be able to see in the prospect's expression that a decision has been made. Many times what people are thinking will be revealed in their facial expressions. When the prospect has the look of having made a decision, it is time to close.

Body Language The prospect's body language might tell you that a decision to buy has been reached. Some of the body movements to look for include rising from the chair and walking to the window, heel-tapping or ear-pulling, looking at the product or model of the product again, looking at the proposal form or the contract again, picking up the phone to call an administrative assistant about some nonessential matter, or nodding in agreement that the product is the best item to meet the prospect's needs.

Recognition Statements Statements by the prospect that your company offers excellent on-time delivery, that local suppliers such as your com-

---

THE PROSPECT IS READY TO BUY

When the prospect shows any of the following signals, you can assume a new customer has been found.

- Asking about availability with questions like, "How soon can the product be here?"
- Asking specific questions about rates or prices or making statements about availability
- Asking about features, options, quality, guarantees, or warranties
- Asking positive questions about the company you represent
- Asking for something to be repeated
- Making statements about problems with previous vendors
- Asking about follow-up service or other products you carry
- Asking about other satisfied customers (Be prepared to provide the names and contact information of previous customers.)

5.1 CLOSING AND THE SALES PROCESS

pany are favored, that your product is of the highest quality, or any other statement of this type would be a signal that is it time to close.

Questions Questions about guarantees or contract terms show a strong interest in closing the sale. As this will be important to a customer, be sure that you know this information. You would not want to miss out on a closing opportunity by having to stop and locate this information.

Necessary Requirements If the prospect states requirements for the product, such as the importance of on-time delivery, training, or packaging needs, this is an indication that the sale is being finalized. In the prospect's mind, the product is being used when these requirements are discussed.

CHECKPOINT

What are some reasons that sales do not close?

KEEPING IT LEGAL

A salesperson must act ethically throughout the entire sales process. Sometimes in attempts to close, the salesperson may mislead prospects. The salesperson may be overly enthusiastic and exaggerate the capabilities of the product or may give incorrect information about the competition's product. This could lead to lawsuits against the salesperson's company. A salesperson must always be straightforward with prospects and customers, warn prospects of potential problems involved in using the product, and avoid misrepresenting product or service capabilities, creating unintended warranties, and criticizing the competition. The basic rule in the selling profession is that the customer should be able to rely on what a salesperson says.

Laws are the basis of settling disagreements related to sales situations. The various laws and their court interpretations are relatively clear and understandable. The problem usually arises in determining the facts. Was an offer really made? Was it really accepted? Were the salesperson's statements about a customer slanderous? There is a great deal to learn about the laws related to selling. The areas most likely to involve salespeople—agency contracts, torts, parts of the Universal Commercial Code, consumer protection laws, and antitrust legislation—will be examined in this lesson.

Working in groups, make a list of dishonest acts in which a salesperson might be tempted to participate.

AGENCY CONTRACTS

Salespeople often act as an agent for the company or *principal* whose products they are selling. An *agency relationship* exists when a customer deals with a salesperson representing the principal. The agent's powers to act for the company are defined in the agency agreement between the two. The salesperson usually will have the authority to solicit sales and to negotiate terms

101

within the limits set by the company but will not have the authority to finalize a contract of sale. In an agency relationship, when a salesperson and a customer sign a written order form, it is a formal offer to purchase by the customer. For it to be a contract, the offer must be accepted by the principal.

The customer can cancel the order without penalty at any time before the principal accepts it. If the salesperson does have the authority to make a binding contract, it is important that the customer know that the offer being made is binding.

The salesperson acting as an agent owes the principal loyalty, obedience of instructions, care and skill, and information that is relevant to the sale. The principal should compensate the agent, reimburse the agent for expenses, and cover losses suffered when conducting agency business.

TORTS

Tort is a legal term for any harm done to persons or property that does not arrive out of a contractual relationship. The principal is responsible to third parties for any torts an agent commits while conducting agency business. *Unintentional negligence torts* are those torts that are brought about by negligence. If a salesperson were at fault in a car accident, the damage caused to others would be an unintentional tort. Intentional torts include libel, slander, assault and battery, false imprisonment, and fraud.

CONTRACTS

Agreements, binding by law, that determine the rights and duties of the contracting parties are called **contracts**. Contract law applies to the legal rights of buyers and sellers that guide the nature and specifics of the transaction.

Modern interpretations of contract law are contained in the Uniform Commercial Code and other areas of the law. When you have a contract signed by all parties involved, if one party does not perform according to his or her responsibilities, the other party can bring legal action for damages.

Not all agreements are contracts. As previously discussed, in an agency contract, an offer to buy is only a negotiation between two parties and does not ordinarily become a contract until it is accepted by the principal. In order for an agreement to be a contract, it must involve legally competent parties, offer and acceptance, consideration, and legal subject matter.

Legally Competent Parties People in certain legally defined conditions are not bound by contracts. These conditions include mental incapacity and minority. A person may lack mental capacity for a number of reasons, such as unsound mind, senility, and a certain state of drunkenness. Contracts with minors are voidable by the minor, except for contracts involving the necessities of life, but they can be enforced against the seller. This has important implications in sales. For example, a minor could buy an item that is not necessary for life, use it, and then bring it back to the seller and demand full return of the purchase price.

Offer and Acceptance An offer is a proposal of the terms for entering into a contract. A proposal that lacks the essentials of an offer may not serve

5.1 CLOSING AND THE SALES PROCESS

as the basis for forming a contract. These essentials are an intent to contract, reasonably clear terms, and legal communication of the terms to the offeree. An offer may be revoked by the offerer or nullified by the passing of a specified or a reasonable time. If any changes are made in the offer, it becomes a new offer. Acceptance must be made without reservation. The acceptance must be either explicitly expressed or implied by the actions of the offeree.

Consideration Consideration is the giving up of some legal right. If Sally agrees to pay Sonny, and Sonny says he appreciates it, there is no consideration on Sonny's part. However, if Sonny promises to do a stated amount of work in return for Sally's payment, there is consideration.

Legal Subject Matter If an agreement involves intent to violate public law, or if performance involves breaking the law or is deemed by the court to go against public policy, the agreement is illegal and, therefore, unenforceable.

THE UNIFORM COMMERCIAL CODE (UCC)

Article 2 of the UCC deals with sales. It applies only to the sale of personal property, not to real estate. The Uniform Commercial Code

- Distinguishes between a sale of goods and such related matters as contracts to sell, bailments, options of purchase, conditional sales, and gifts.

- Makes specific provisions regarding offer and acceptance and determination of unclear or unstated provisions of the sale agreement.

- Requires that the contract be in writing and observe other formalities when the sale price is $500 or more.

- Makes provisions as to actual time of transfer of title under various circumstances and who bears the risk of damage or loss of the goods for the time period between execution of the sales contract and actual physical possession of goods by the purchaser.

- Sets out the rights and duties of each party with regard to the seller's duty to deliver and the buyer's duty to accept the goods and with regard to the transportation of goods under various contract provisions.

- Makes provisions regarding performance of the goods and the seller's warranties.

In 1978, the UCC was modified to allow certain alterations to contracts to fit modern business conditions. Terms not specified by exchange partners may be agreed to and incorporated into contracts even after the contract has been formed. A contract can also be concluded even though price, place of delivery, time of performance, and other particulars are unsettled. The UCC allows unforeseen circumstances to be taken into consideration to account for those situations in which parties cannot carry out contracted obligations. Delay or nondelivery is not considered a breach when the agreed-upon carrier becomes unavailable and a substitute is used. If a customer rejects a delivery not in accordance with the original agreement, the seller has the right to make a conforming delivery before the contract time expires. When the planned form of payment is impossible, equivalent means of payment is allowed. When a buyer fails to make a purchase in accordance with a contractual obligation, the seller may resell the goods at a private or public sale.

CONSUMER PROTECTION LAWS

A variety of laws and government agencies protect the public against harmful products. You will have to be sure that the products you sell meet all consumer protection standards.

The Federal Food, Drug, and Cosmetic Act bans the sale of impure, improperly labeled, falsely guaranteed, and unhealthy foods, drugs, and cosmetics. The Food and Drug Administration (FDA) enforces this law. The FDA has the power to force producers to stop manufacturing products that are unsafe.

The Consumer Product Safety Act of 1972 sets safety standards for products other than food and drugs. When the Consumer Product Safety Commission determines that a product is unsafe, it can make businesses recall and stop selling the product.

Antitrust Legislation Beginning in 1890, laws were created that made *monopolies* in certain industries illegal. A monopoly, or exclusive control over a commercial activity, is also called a trust, and these laws were called *antitrust laws*. Antitrust laws also ban other types of business activities that do not promote competition. It is important to become familiar with these laws so that you do not do anything illegal. The Antitrust Division of the Justice Department and the Federal Trade Commission are two government agencies that make sure competition remains fair.

ANTITRUST LEGISLATION

1. **Sherman Act** Makes it illegal for competitors to get together and set prices on the products or services they sell. This means that you and your competitors cannot decide together to keep prices at a certain level. Discussing prices with competitors is illegal.

2. **Clayton Act** States that it is illegal for a business to require a customer to purchase one good in order to be able to purchase another good. For example, a distributor of computers cannot make customers purchase software when they purchase a computer. Customers must be free to buy only the products or services they want.

3. **Robinson-Patman Act** Makes it illegal to charge different prices to different groups of nonretail customers. If you own a retail store, you can charge different prices to different customers, such as giving discounts to senior citizens. If your business sells to other businesses, you must offer the same terms to all those businesses.

4. **Wheeler-Lea Act** Bans unfair or deceptive actions or practices by businesses. False advertising is an example. Under the Wheeler-Lea Act, businesses are also required to tell consumers about possible negative features of their products. Drug companies, for example, must let people know about any side effects they may experience from using a medication.

PROHIBITED ACTS

The common law, criminal and civil statutes, and antitrust and consumer protection laws specifically prohibit certain acts that might arise in selling activities. New salespeople should be given specific information and training concerning the illegal activities most likely to occur in their situation. In addition to obeying the antitrust laws discussed previously, salespeople must be

5.1 CLOSING AND THE SALES PROCESS

professional and avoid misrepresentation, fraud, collusion, bribes, false labeling, price discrimination, tie-in sales, exclusive dealerships, and reciprocity.

Misrepresentation If the seller has misstated a fact that is significant in the buying decision, the buyer, under contract law, can cancel the sale. This may be true even if the seller was not aware of the misrepresentation.

Fraud Fraud involves willfully misrepresenting a material fact to another person with the intention of causing the person to enter into a contract. If the other person is legally entitled to rely on the truth of the statement and enters into a contract to his or her detriment, fraud has been committed. The injured party may void the sale, and damages may be awarded under a tort action.

Collusion Collusion involves two or more people conspiring together and acting to the detriment of another person. The Sherman Act prohibits collusion between sellers that results in price fixing or in dividing territories on a noncompeting basis. The Federal Trade Commission works against an even broader range of collusive activities.

Bribes Bribing is using money or favors to persuade someone to do something. Certain bribes may violate civil or criminal law, depending on the nature of the so-called extra incentive.

False Labeling Changing or falsifying the label on a food or drug item is in violation of the Pure Food and Drug Act. In other cases, false labeling might be held to be illegal as fraud.

Price Discrimination Price discrimination occurs when buyers of equal circumstances are charged unequal prices or given unequal terms for identical purchases. The Robinson-Patman Act makes this practice illegal under certain circumstances. Salespeople should know what these circumstances are in their particular industry.

Tie-In Sales When the demand for a product is so strong that the seller is able to require the buyer to order a second, unwanted product in connection with the purchase of the first product, it is called a tie-in sale. The Clayton Act prohibits tie-in sales when they substantially lessen competition. This involves a question of fact in each case. Salespeople should be knowledgeable about tie-in sales as they relate to their industry.

Exclusive Dealerships A contract that limits a wholesaler or retailer to handling the product of only one manufacturer is an exclusive dealing contract. The Clayton Act prohibits this kind of contract when it substantially lessens competition.

Reciprocity Reciprocity is a concept that means "I'll buy from you if you buy from me." When these agreements lessen competition, they are in violation of the Clayton Act.

COMMUNICATE

Ethical behavior is important to salespeople. A Code of Ethics established by a company is a set of ethical guidelines that employees are expected to follow. Some salespeople develop a personal Code of Ethics. Develop a Code of Ethics for yourself that you could follow if you were employed as a salesperson. Share this code with your class.

CHECKPOINT

Why does a salesperson need to know the laws related to the sales process?

_____
_____

CHAPTER 5 CLOSING AND BEYOND

THINK CRITICALLY

1. What must you do to reach the goal of every sales presentation?

2. Why are salespeople sometimes afraid to ask a prospect for an order?

3. What four components must be present in order for an agreement to be a contract?

4. What is the purpose of laws that relate to selling?

5. What are some signals the salesperson should look for in determining the proper time to close?

6. Why has it been necessary to modify the Uniform Commercial Code?

MAKE CONNECTIONS

7. **RESEARCH** Using the library or the Internet, research product liability lawsuits that have been in the news recently and analyze the effect they have had on the companies involved.

8. **COMMUNICATION** With a partner, role play a sales meeting, demonstrating the body language of a prospect who does not want to close and one who is ready to close.

9. **RESEARCH** Research one of the laws involved in the sales process. Prepare a one-page report on the history of the law and its current effect on sales.

LESSON 5.2
METHODS OF CLOSING

EXPLAIN the strategies that are used to lead prospects to closing

IDENTIFY basic closing methods

ANALYZE options when the answer is "no"

EXPLAIN why unprofessional closing methods should not be used

ASKING FOR ACTION

In order to lead a prospect to closing, a salesperson might use the technique of assuming the prospect will agree or the technique of remaining silent. Successful salespeople have used both techniques with good results.

ASSUMING THE PROSPECT WILL AGREE

Once you have spent time and effort working with a prospect to diagnose needs and you have proposed a good solution to those needs, you can assume the prospect will agree with you and choose to purchase your product or service. You can communicate this assumption in several ways.

Being energetic To show energy, sit forward in your chair, and talk a little faster and louder than normal.

ON THE $CENE

After meeting with his manager, Runjan had some ideas on how to close sales. The next presentation he made went very smoothly. He discussed with the prospect her need for a reliable, fast, networkable copier. Runjan helped her understand how easy it would be for employees to send jobs to the copier from their workstations and eliminate lines and wasted time at the copier. The prospect agreed with all of Runjan's selling points and eagerly signed the sales order when Runjan presented it to her. Why do you think Runjan was able to close the sale so easily this time?

CHAPTER 5 CLOSING AND BEYOND

TECHNOLOGY AND TRADE SHOWS Trade shows are an opportunity for vendors to display and demonstrate products for interested prospects. Companies are incorporating technology into their trade show exhibits in a variety of ways. Some companies give attendees a chance to preview their offerings online before the trade show begins. This increases the chance that they will stop by the exhibit at the trade show. Other companies have integrated multimedia technology into their exhibits to give attendees an opportunity to take a virtual tour of their manufacturing facilities.

THINK CRITICALLY What are the advantages of utilizing technology in trade shows?

Being confident and positive Avoid expressions that communicate uncertainty. Speak like you expect the prospect to agree with you. Talk about *when* they use the product, not *if* they use it.

Speaking clearly and with enthusiasm Be enthusiastic about your product. If the prospect thinks you are excited about the product, your enthusiasm likely will be catching. Always speak clearly. Even if you have made the pitch many times before, do not let the prospect know this. Remember, this is the *first time* this prospect has heard it.

USING SILENCE

Once you ask the prospect for an order, be quiet. Wait for the prospect to respond no matter how long it takes. This will give the prospect time to

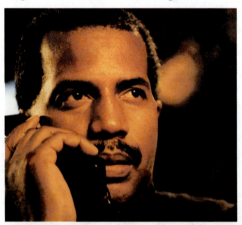

think. It can also make the prospect uncomfortable and put pressure on the prospect to end the silence. This technique is used when the buying decision in terms of price and impact on the prospect is significant. However, silence is not always a good approach because it forces a "yes" or "no" answer, and this often leads to objections. Silence also does not allow the salesperson an opportunity to help the prospect make the decision.

CHECKPOINT ✓

What are two strategies that have been used to lead prospects to closing?

5.2 METHODS OF CLOSING

BASIC CLOSING APPROACHES

A professional salesperson selects the closing method that best fits the prospect and the selling method. Questioning is important in all closing methods because questions require answers. As the prospect answers each question, it should help move him or her toward a commitment to buy.

The *trial close* tests to see how far along the prospect has come toward the buying decision. The testing can take the form of a question or a statement. If the response from the prospect is positive, it may signal that it is time to close. If the response is not positive, it is the salesperson's signal that the prospect needs more information. A successful salesperson is persistent. If you believe that your product will solve a problem for a prospect, you should not give up until every possible means of encouragement to buy has been explored. Zig Ziglar says that the most successful salespeople give prospects at least five opportunities to make a specific buying decision. The highest percentage of closes comes on the last offer.

did you KNOW?

According to a survey conducted by a professor at Notre Dame University, 4 percent of the salespeople in America earn 60 percent of the money.

DIRECT REQUEST

The **direct request** closing method involves a request for the prospect to place the order immediately. As the sales process has changed over the years, this method has come to be viewed as a high-pressure tactic. An example of the direct request is, "Mr. Jackson, can you think of anything else we should talk about? If not, then give me your authorization right here, and I'll get this copier set up and ready to go." The words used are direct and to the point, and they emphasize that a binding contract is being entered into.

INDIRECT REQUEST

The **indirect request** closing method involves behavior by the salesperson based on the assumption that the prospect has decided to buy. This method is commonly used in retail sales and in other situations in which the impact of deciding to buy is not going to have a tremendous effect on the prospect. You can help a prospect make a decision by asking a question like, "Will this be cash or charge?" The prospect does not have to say "yes" and is immediately involved in decisions that would be made after the sale.

IMPENDING EVENT

The **impending event** closing method involves stressing to the prospect that the decision to buy should be made now because something may happen soon that will make a delay costly. The event that might occur will vary from industry to industry. Some of the impending events that might make a delay costly to the prospect include a change in price, a rise in interest rates, a change in delivery and shipping terms, changes in political and economic

ALWAYS BE PREPARED FOR A MEETING

Most of your sales meetings will be planned in advance, but there will be occasions when you have to make an unexpected call on a company. You can be prepared for any meeting if you always have the following items with you.

- Customer data
- Brochures and samples
- Business cards
- Order forms
- Paper and pens
- Calculator
- Map of your territory
- Appointment calendar
- Emergency clothing items (tie for men and hosiery for women)

Working in small groups, brainstorm a list of products to be sold and decide which closing method would work best for each product and why.

conditions, and the weather. Using this method, the salesperson might say to a prospect, "These cars are manufactured and shipped to us from Detroit, and since this is the only one we have in stock and a major blizzard is predicted for Detroit, it could be weeks before another model like this one will be available."

SUMMARY OF BENEFITS

The **summary of benefits** method involves restating benefits the customer will receive from the product or service. It is a way to summarize the features and benefits of the product and show how it will meet the prospect's needs. It is usually done to recap the problem-solving phase in order to establish the proper perspective on the recommended solution. For example, after introducing the features and benefits of a product, the salesperson could use the summary of benefits method and say to the prospect, "Mr. Jackson, you stated that you need a copier that will eliminate wait times, allow workers to send documents to the copier from their workstations, and make quality copies of color photos. This copier is exactly what you need."

NARROWING THE CHOICE

The **narrowing the choice** closing method repeats the part of the process when alternatives are considered. This step is closely related to the *solving the problem* step of the sales process. Alternatives are eliminated until the best alternative is identified. An example of this method would be to say to the prospect, "Mr. Jackson, you want a copier that will make quality copies of color photos. The first two models we looked at make color copies, but this third model is the top of the line for copying color photos."

SPECIAL OFFER

The **special offer** closing method involves offering the prospect a special offer for a *limited time only*. The offer can be withdrawn at any time or can be for a specific length of time. This closing method gives the prospect a reason for acting immediately. A salesperson should handle special offers carefully. If it is done too often, prospects may not buy until a special offer is made. Making an offer like the following is an example of the special offer: "Mr. Jackson, if you purchase this copier today, I can offer you free toner for six months."

STANDING ROOM ONLY

The **standing room only** (SRO) closing method suggests to the prospect that the product or service may not be available later. The SRO method is widely used in advertising. Like the special offer method, the SRO method

5.2 METHODS OF CLOSING

encourages the prospect to act immediately. If too much time is taken to decide, the prospect may miss the chance to buy. When using this method, the salesperson might say to the prospect, "Mr. Jackson, this copier is available at this price because this model is being upgraded. We only have two machines in stock at this price, and I need to tell you that I have three other appointments this afternoon. Don't miss out on this chance. It's a great buy!"

Why do salespeople use different closing approaches?
_____
_____

WHEN THE ANSWER IS NO

The best salespeople with the best presentations will sometimes get "no" for an answer. As discussed earlier in this chapter, a negative response may be a salesperson's signal to redirect the presentation and be sure the prospect sees how needs can be met by the product. But sometimes "no" will really mean "no," and it is the salesperson's signal to move on to another prospect.

THANK YOU

The salesperson should thank the prospect for the opportunity of making the presentation. If the prospect is agreeable, the salesperson should try to get some feedback from the prospect as to why the decision was made not to buy, what the product lacked in features and benefits, and what the salesperson did or did not do that would have helped the sale.

WALKING AWAY

A successful salesperson knows when to give up on a sale. After exploring the needs of a prospect, if the salesperson realizes that there is no match between the product and the prospect's needs, the sale should be abandoned. However, if the salesperson sees the chance for future business, contact should be maintained with the prospect. It should not be regular follow-up contact, but when something comes along that is truly relevant to the prospect's needs, the salesperson should share it with the prospect.

What are the advantages of walking away from some sales?
_____
_____

111

UNPROFESSIONAL CLOSINGS

When customer satisfaction and relationship building are important, some closing methods should be avoided. These methods are unprofessional and often use high-pressure techniques.

EMOTIONAL CLOSE

The *emotional close* seeks to get prospects so excited that their emotions force them into buying. This is not really a closing method. It is a motivation technique that works the prospect into a highly emotional state just before closing. This method is not very effective and is considered unprofessional by successful salespeople. Informed prospects know from experience that decisions should not be made until their emotions are calm and they can make a reasonable decision.

GIVE-UP CLOSE

In the *give-up close* method, the salesperson acts as if there is no point in continuing the sales presentation. The prospect then relaxes, thinking that the salesperson has given up on making a sale. At this point, the salesperson makes a very forceful closing. This method involves deception on the part of the salesperson.

An experienced prospect will resent this approach. The salesperson can take a more professional approach by discussing the difficulty of decision making with the prospect and reviewing the sales proposal with the prospect rather than acting like the sales opportunity is over.

SHOWDOWN CLOSE

The *showdown close* is a buy-now-or-miss-out-on-the-opportunity version of the direct closing method. Rarely is this method justified. In this approach, the salesperson tells the prospect that unless an order is placed, the meeting is over and there will be no more opportunities for the prospect to do business with the salesperson.

Describe unprofessional closing methods.

5.2 **METHODS OF CLOSING**

THINK CRITICALLY

1. If the salesperson assumes the prospect will agree, why does this help lead to a successful closing?

2. Why is silence not always a good approach for closing?

3. What is the purpose of a trial close?

4. If you were selling scooters for children and you wanted to overcome the safety fears of the parents, which closing method would you use? How would you attempt to close the sale?

5. Why do you think some salespeople use unprofessional closing methods?

6. Why should a salesperson avoid using an unprofessional closing method?

MAKE CONNECTIONS

7. **RESEARCH** Interview a professional salesperson. Find out what techniques the salesperson uses to close a sale. Prepare a report of your findings and present it to your class.

8. **COMMUNICATION** Choose one of the closing methods. With a partner, role play a sales situation with one of you acting as the salesperson and the other acting as the prospect. Demonstrate the closing method. Choose another method and switch roles.

9. **RESEARCH** Search the Internet for information on trade shows. Make a list of companies that you find that have trade show information on the Internet.

113

LESSON 5.3
AFTER THE SALE

EXPLAIN the importance of follow-up activities

IDENTIFY efficient time-management techniques for salespeople

EXPLAIN techniques to help when sales are slow

CUSTOMER FOLLOW-UP

As a salesperson, it will be important for you to make your customers feel that their business is appreciated. Customers need to know that you will be there after the sale is completed. If the only time customers hear from you is when you want their order, they will not feel that you value their business. *Customer follow-up* helps salespeople establish long-term relationships with customers by constantly looking for ways to assist them. Become a valuable resource for customers. Look for information customers would be interested in and drop it off at their office or mail it to them with a note. Follow-up activities that can be beneficial to relationship-building include letters, visits, service, gifts and entertainment, and a variety of other thoughtful acts.

ON THE $CENE

Runjan was having much more success on sales calls now that he had overcome his fear of closing. Now his biggest problem was finding time to finish all of the required reports and correspondence. He began each day knowing what he needed to do, but somehow by the end of the day, none of his paperwork had been finished. If he got to an appointment early, he would find a local coffee shop or bookstore and relax and read some sports magazines while waiting for the time to pass. What do you think Runjan should be doing during this downtime?

5.3 AFTER THE SALE

FOLLOW-UP LETTER

The letter written to a prospect after a sales meeting is an opportunity for you to accomplish two things. It allows you to thank the prospect for taking time to meet with you. It also gives you a chance to summarize the points you made during the meeting and remind the prospect how your product can solve problems. If any follow-up activity was discussed, restate it in the letter.

Be sure to take notes during or immediately after a sales meeting. These notes will help keep you organized. Otherwise, by the end of a day, you will not remember what was discussed with each prospect. With today's technology, it is easy to keep your notes and send correspondence to prospects. If you write and store a file with the body of a standard follow-up letter, you can merge it with information from your prospect database, add some customized information, and quickly have the letter ready to go.

You should also write a thank you note to customers when a sale is made. This should be the beginning of a variety of follow-up activities that you conduct. Always include your business card with every letter and note that you send to customers.

SAMPLE FOLLOW-UP LETTER

August 21, 2002

Mr. Joe Seawright
123 Greenwood Street
Abbeville, GA 30001

Dear Mr. Seawright

Thanks so much for meeting with me last week for the demonstration of our new T3000 Network Copier. This copier is the answer for all of your business needs. Employees will be able to send their large or small copying jobs to the copier from their workstations and pick it up when it is convenient. The T3000 prints in color or black and white at the rate of 100 pages per minute. There will be no more waiting in line at the copier, and no more of your employees' valuable time will be wasted!

If you have any questions about the proposal I left with you, please contact me at (404) 555-3000. I will check with you at the end of the week to set up a final meeting.

Thanks again for your valuable time.

Sincerely

Runjan Jain
Sales Associate

FOLLOW-UP VISITS

Once prospects become customers, you should continue to keep in touch with them. Drop by their businesses just to make sure everything is going well with their use of your products. This reassures customers that you are concerned with their satisfaction and not just with making a sale. This will also keep you fresh in their minds when it comes time to place more orders.

BUSINESS CARD ETIQUETTE

The business card is a very important tool for doing business overseas. When presented in written form, your name may be easier for others to understand. Also, some countries place more emphasis on rank and profession. Here are some suggestions regarding the use of business cards in other countries.

- Include your company name and your title on your business card.
- Do not use abbreviations as these may be unfamiliar to others.
- If you are going to a country where most natives do not speak English, consider having your information translated into the language of the country and printed on the reverse side of your business card.
- In most of Southeast Asia, Africa, and the Middle East, you should never present your business card with your left hand.
- When doing business in Japan, use both hands to present your business card, and be sure the type is right side up and facing the recipient.

THINK CRITICALLY When doing business in other countries, why should you follow the customs of that country relating to business cards?

If the customer is not available when you drop in, leave your business card to show that you were there and that you have an interest in their continued satisfaction. Be sure your business card has all of your contact information on it, including any phone numbers they can use to reach you—office, fax, and cell phone—and any e-mail addresses you use. Make it easy for your customers to contact you.

SERVICE

Some products will require more service than others. As a salesperson, you will need to know how much service the product you are selling will require. If another department in your company performs the service, be sure customers know whom to contact. If possible, introduce customers to service personnel at the time the sale is made. You should check with customers periodically to see that service is being handled correctly. If the product requires little or no service, then check with customers periodically to see that the product is performing well. For example, if you sell cars, take customers to the service department and introduce them to the service writers and some of the automotive technicians after they purchase a new car. When they need service, they will know whom to contact and will be more comfortable bringing their car back for service.

5.3 AFTER THE SALE

GIFTS AND ENTERTAINMENT

Gifts frequently are offered in appreciation for a sale, and salespeople often entertain prospects and customers during the sales process. You should always practice ethical behavior and be sure that the gifts and entertainment you offer are appropriate. Sending a box of candy or a flower arrangement after a customer has made a major purchase, such as an automobile, is a nice gesture and shows customers that you appreciate their business.

Remember also to thank customers for their referrals of other prospects. If the referral results in a sale for you, you should send the customer a gift. Again, be sure the gift is appropriate for the value of the referral.

NEWSLETTER

If your company sends a newsletter to customers, be sure to contribute articles to the newsletter to keep your name in front of your customers. If your company does not have a newsletter, make your own. Include articles about new products and services offered by your company and other topics of general interest to customers.

Desktop publishing and word processing software offer an inexpensive way for individuals to keep in touch with customers and prospects. You can create a professional newsletter in a short amount of time using software packages. Many packages have built-in templates that make layout and design easy. You can also insert photos, including photos of customers if you wish. You might consider inviting customers to submit information for your newsletter.

OTHER THOUGHTFUL ACTIVITIES

Take time to recognize events in your customers' lives. Send greeting cards for birthdays, anniversaries, births, and other major accomplishments when you learn about them. The use of a *tickler file*—a file organized by dates—will be especially helpful to remind you of these events. Many computer organizers have built-in reminder functions that would help you remember these occasions.

Why is follow-up of sales important?

ORGANIZING FOR SUCCESS

Managing time efficiently can be a challenge. Once you begin working as a salesperson, you will develop your own procedures for handling the variety of required tasks. The following information will be helpful as you begin a career in sales.

PLANNING SALES CALLS

You must know where your sales territory is so that you can *route* or list your calls orderly and productively for a sales trip. Once you have planned your route, you need to schedule appointments efficiently.

When scheduling appointments, remember that densely populated urban areas will require more of your time than smaller rural areas. Also, remember to schedule time to check in with established customers you have in the area.

Be sure to allow adequate time for each appointment so you do not appear rushed when meeting with prospects. As a courtesy to prospects, be a few minutes early, so you do not keep them waiting. If they have to wait too long, they might decide they do not have time to see you.

MAKE EFFICIENT USE OF DOWNTIME

When traveling and waiting for appointments, there is the potential for a lot of wasted time. You should always keep professional journals and reports

BUSINESS MATH CONNECTION

Salespeople often are required to travel for their jobs, and companies usually reimburse travel expenses. To receive a reimbursement, the salesperson must calculate expenses and submit an expense report to the company. If Vicki traveled for four nights and had $125 in total meal expenses, $108 per night in lodging, and 325 miles in mileage, which her company reimburses at the rate of $0.34 per mile, what are her total travel expenses?

SOLUTION
To calculate mileage expenses, multiply the number of miles by the reimbursement rate per mile.

325 miles × $0.34 per mile = $110.50

Multiply nightly lodging charges by the number of nights.

$108 × 4 nights = $432.00

Add mileage, lodging, and meal expenses to calculate the total.

$110.50 + $432.00 + $125.00 = $667.50

5.3 AFTER THE SALE

you are working on in your briefcase. When you see that you are going to have some downtime, you will be able to use the time to read journals in your field or work on required reports. Laptop computers have made this very easy to do.

You can also use the time to make telephone calls to confirm other appointments or to make follow-up calls. Some businesses have a telephone available in the waiting area for their guests, or your company may give you a cell phone to use to stay in touch with prospects and customers.

ADMINISTRATIVE TASKS

Sales reports, correspondence, and expense reports need to be completed in a timely manner. If you have a laptop computer, you can take care of these reports when you are on the road or at home. You might need to schedule one day a week or certain days each month in the office to take care of these tasks.

Telephone calls and e-mails should be answered as soon as possible. If you are away from your office, make it a point to check your voice mail and e-mail during the day. You do not want to miss out on an order because you did not return a phone call.

USING A CALENDAR

A calendar or personal organizer will be helpful to you in scheduling efficient use of your time. Whether you use a large page-per-month calendar, a yearly planning calendar, or a pocket-sized calendar, you need to record all upcoming events on it as soon as you learn of them.

You can use your calendar to plan your "to do list" each day. A "to do list" is an effective way to plan your daily work. At the end of your day, make a list of all the tasks you need to complete the next day. Prioritize the tasks from the most important to the least important. The next day, mark off each task as it is completed. At the end of the day, transfer any tasks that are not completed to the "to do list" for the next day.

WORKSHOP

Working in small groups, make a list of uses for a calendar for a salesperson.

Why is efficient use of time important for a salesperson?

_____

_____

SURVIVING SLOW TIMES

When the economy is going well, it is easy for a salesperson to stop trying new sales techniques and to get into a pattern with customers where their needs are not analyzed regularly. When the economy takes a down turn and sales are slow, you need to take time to refamiliarize yourself with your customers. You should call on them without trying to sell anything.

Customers are a company's best source of product information. If you listen carefully to your customers, you will get valuable information to share with your product development department. Help them stay a step ahead and develop products that customers want.

STAY MOTIVATED
Try to maintain a positive attitude when sales are slow. Listen to motivational tapes and read motivational books to stay focused. Try some new selling techniques. You might find one that works better than what you were previously using.

GOAL SETTING
As a salesperson, you should always set goals. During slow times, be realistic about goals you can reach. If you were selling $200,000 of merchandise per quarter during good economic times, don't expect to reach that same goal in slower times. Shorten the timeframe on your goals. If you are setting quarterly, half-yearly, and yearly goals during good economic times, focus your efforts on shorter time periods, such as daily, weekly, and monthly goals.

SAVE FOR SLOW TIMES
During prosperous times when your commission checks are large, deposit money in a savings account, certificate of deposit, or other safe investment. Then when times are slow, you will have money to fall back on and will not have to lower your standard of living.

WORK WITH OTHERS
Working with other salespeople in your company can be a great source of ideas. Brainstorm with team members on ideas for the sales process. Everyone has a different approach to selling, and you might find some new ideas that will work for you. You can also share objections heard from customers and responses that are effective. Everyone calls on different customers and hears different objections. Sharing these can help you be better prepared.

What are some techniques for surviving the slow times in selling?

THINK CRITICALLY

1. What is the purpose of a follow-up letter after a sales call?

2. After a sale is made, what does a follow-up visit to a customer accomplish?

3. Why is sending cards to customers on holidays and for special events a good form of follow-up?

4. Why is it important for a salesperson not to waste time when making sales calls?

5. Why do you think it is easy for a salesperson to get discouraged when the economy slows?

MAKE CONNECTIONS

6. **COMMUNICATION** Write a follow-up letter that you could send to a prospect after a sales call. Use word processing software and format the document as a business letter.

7. **BUSINESS MATH** Marsha went on a five-night sales trip. She had the following expenses. What is the total of her expenses?

    Lodging: $112.42 each night

    Meals: $32.00 each day

    Mileage: 425 miles at $0.34 per mile

    Entertainment of Clients: $220

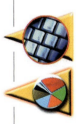

8. **RESEARCH** Using the Internet or other resources, locate information on software packages that help salespeople organize customer data. Make a chart or design a poster comparing the features of the different packages. Present your findings to your class.

REVIEW

CHAPTER SUMMARY

LESSON 5.1 Closing and the Sales Process
A. The goal of every sales presentation is to close the sale. Sometimes a sale does not close because of the salesperson's fears of closing or because of problems in the development of the sales process.
B. As a company representative, a salesperson must always display ethical behavior. Laws are used to settle disagreements related to sales situations. Salespeople must stay current on laws affecting their industry.

LESSON 5.2 Methods of Closing
A. Salespeople use different approaches to lead prospects to closing such as assuming the prospect will agree and maintaining silence.
B. Closing methods include direct request, summary of benefits, narrowing the choice, special offer, and standing room only.
C. Sometimes the prospect will not be convinced to buy. The salesperson must realize when to walk away and move on to the next prospect.
D. Some salespeople use unprofessional closing methods that put undue pressure or fear in the prospect. Ethical salespeople do not use these.

LESSON 5.3 After the Sale
A. Follow-up letters, follow-up visits, service, gifts and entertainment, and notes and holiday cards are all effective methods of follow up.
B. Time management is important for salespeople. Planning sales calls and making efficient use of downtime are part of a salesperson's job.
C. Economic times change, and sales will not always be good. A salesperson must be able to survive the slow times as well as the good times.

VOCABULARY BUILDER

Choose the term that best fits the definition. Write the letter of the answer in the space provided. Some terms may not be used.

____ 1. Request made based on assumption that the prospect has decided to buy

____ 2. Request for prospect to place the order immediately

____ 3. Agreement, binding by law, that determines the rights and duties of involved parties

____ 4. Customer's acceptance of the product or service you are selling and the purchase of it

____ 5. Restating benefits the customer will receive from the product or service

____ 6. Stresses to the prospect that something may happen in the future that will make delayed purchase costly

____ 7. Suggests that the product or service may not be available later

a. closing
b. contract
c. direct request
d. impending event
e. indirect request
f. narrowing the choice
g. special offer
h. standing room only
i. summary of benefits

CHAPTER 5

REVIEW CONCEPTS

8. When does the closing process begin?

9. What are some things a salesperson can do to overcome closing fears?

10. What types of problems can occur in the development of the sales process that can cause a sale not to close?

11. What areas of the law are most likely to involve salespeople?

12. Where can interpretations of contract law be found?

13. What is the purpose of consumer protection laws?

14. Explain the acts that a salesperson is prohibited from doing.

15. Summarize the differences between the direct request and the summary of benefits closing methods.

POINT YOUR BROWSER

b2000.swep.com

REVIEW

16. Summarize the differences between the special offer and standing room only closing methods.

17. Why is service after a sale an important part of the sales process?

18. How can salespeople make good use of downtime?

19. What could be the effect of a salesperson failing to take care of administrative tasks?

20. Why would setting goals help a salesperson through the slow times?

APPLY WHAT YOU LEARNED

21. You are meeting with a prospect and are approaching the end of your presentation. The prospect begins pulling her ear and tapping her feet. She appears restless and reaches for the product sample on the table. You continue through the remainder of your presentation and then decide to review the features and benefits of the product again. What did you do wrong?

22. You are traveling from one sales appointment to another in your own personal vehicle. On a day between appointments, you decide to take the day off and spend it at the beach. While at the beach, you are driving on the highway when your cell phone rings. You are distracted, and your car crosses the center line and strikes an oncoming vehicle. The driver of the car is injured. What type of law did you break?

CHAPTER 5

23. You are attempting to sell a car to a prospect. He has obtained information from the Internet about the cost of the car and does not want to pay more than 5 percent above cost. You look at the information, and it is correct. However, you do not tell the prospect this and quote him the price you will take, which is 20 percent over cost. When he insists on the 5 percent amount, you become angry and tell him there is no point in continuing this discussion. Is this a good closing method? Why or why not?

_____
_____
_____

24. Why is customer follow-up as important as each of the steps in the sales process?

_____
_____
_____

25. Describe the importance of organizational skills for a salesperson.

_____
_____
_____

MAKE CONNECTIONS

26. **RESEARCH** Using the Internet, research state and local consumer protection laws and analyze their effect on selling. Prepare a written report of your findings.

27. **PROBLEM SOLVING** You have been hired as a designer and salesperson for an interior design store. You realize that customer follow-up will help you build a client base. Decide what follow-up activities you will conduct. Using word processing software, prepare an outline of your follow-up plan.

28. **BUSINESS MATH** Use a spreadsheet to calculate the expenses for Rafael's last sales trip. He was on the road for six nights and traveled 523 miles. Expenses include the following.

    Nightly lodging charges were $98.56 for three nights.

    Nightly lodging charges were $112.45 for two nights.

    Nightly lodging charges were $169.56 for one night.

    Total meal expenses were $197.45.

    Entertainment expenses for clients were $184.50.

    Mileage is reimbursed at the rate of $0.36 per mile.

29. **COMMUNICATION** With a partner, role play a sales meeting from beginning to closing. Present this scenario to your classmates.

125

CHAPTER 6

RETAIL SELLING

LESSONS

6.1 BASICS OF RETAIL SELLING

6.2 SALES PROCESS IN RETAIL SELLING

6.3 OTHER SKILLS FOR RETAIL SELLING

CAREERS IN SELLING

THE HOME DEPOT

With more than 1,000 stores in the western hemisphere, The Home Depot is the world's largest home improvement retailer, offering more than 50,000 products to do-it-yourselfers and professionals. Career advancement primarily occurs from internal applicants.

The Home Depot Merchandising Assistant Store Manager (MASM) manages two or more departments and interacts with customers and associates. The MASM's major responsibilities are implementing business tactics that sell products, opening and closing the store, managing departments, providing and inspiring outstanding service, and leading others to build a team that achieves results. The MASM trains, coaches, and develops and hires associates when necessary.

Internal candidates must have a satisfactory performance rating as a merchandising department supervisor, and external candidates must have five years' management experience in lumber, lighting, plumbing, and hardware and one year's supervisory experience in a retail business.

THINK CRITICALLY

1. Why do you think experience is necessary for the MASM?
2. Do you think you could perform well in this position?

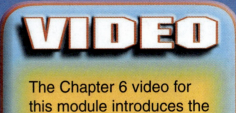

The Chapter 6 video for this module introduces the concepts in this chapter.

PROJECT
Retail Selling Process

PROJECT OBJECTIVES
- Develop an understanding of the retail customer
- Explore the three phases of the sales process in retail selling
- Develop skills in handling activities after the sale

GETTING STARTED
Read through the Project Process below. Make a list of any materials you will need. Decide how you will get the needed materials or information.
- What retail stores would you go to if you wanted to buy beach wear?
- Other than swimsuits, what items would be needed?

PROJECT PROCESS

Part 1 **LESSON 6.1** Go through the retail sales process as a salesperson in one of the stores you listed in Getting Started. What is the classification of beach wear and accessories? Are they impulse, convenience, shopping, or specialty goods? The customers you will be working with are "just-looking."

Part 2 **LESSON 6.2** Continue developing the sales process by answering the following questions.
- Will you conduct any prospecting activities?
- What type of objections do you think you might encounter?
- What type of approach will you use when a prospect enters your store? How will you determine what clothes to show?
- What will you do if the customers come in a group and they are having trouble coming to any decisions?
- How will you close the sale?

Part 3 **LESSON 6.3** Continue the sales process by using suggestive selling. What additional items will you suggest? Choose a method of payment used by the customer and explain how you will handle it.

CHAPTER REVIEW

Project Wrap-up Choose a partner and role play the sales situation you have described, with you being the salesperson and your partner being the customer.

LESSON 6.1
BASICS OF RETAIL SELLING

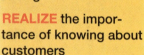

DEVELOP a basic understanding of retail selling

REALIZE the importance of knowing about customers

UNDERSTANDING RETAIL SELLING

Retail selling is different from other selling situations because the prospect comes to the salesperson. Prospects often are emotionally and financially closer to being ready to purchase than many other types of prospects. Interest in the product usually brings the prospect to the retail store. Once in the store, the prospect will have alternatives to consider. The retail salesperson must help the prospect make a decision based on the proper balance between the product, the salesperson, and the retailer. A sale will close if the product fills the customer's need, the salesperson has created an atmosphere of goodwill, and the store is where the customer wants to buy.

CLASSIFICATIONS OF PRODUCTS

It is important for retail salespeople to know how products are classified. The knowledge and skill required of the salesperson will increase with each level of product.

ON THE $CENE

Katie and James liked to go to the local mall and look for items for their new apartment. They noticed that salespeople in some stores appeared more eager to assist customers than those in other stores. Since this was the first time they were buying home furnishings, they preferred to shop where the salespeople offered assistance to them. Do you think most people prefer assistance when shopping?

6.1 BASICS OF RETAIL SELLING

Impulse Goods *Impulse goods* are items bought in haste, with little or no thought as to the wisdom of the purchase. No price or quality comparisons are made at the time of purchase. Examples of impulse goods are magazines, newspapers, popcorn and candy, soft drinks, gum, gadgets, and novelties. Although impulse buying is usually associated with the kinds of goods just mentioned, it can involve an item from any category. Some people might even buy a new car on impulse although we do not usually think of such products as impulse goods. The salesperson has little impact on impulse purchases because they are basically purchased on sight, without much assistance.

Convenience Goods *Convenience goods* are items bought from the most convenient, acceptable retail outlet. Price may influence the choice of the outlet, but the outlet must still be convenient. Because convenience goods are purchased frequently, the buyer usually feels knowledgeable about them. Most items purchased at convenience stores (Quik Trip, Stop 'n Go) are examples of convenience goods. Just as with impulse goods, the salesperson has little impact on convenience purchases other than indicating where goods are located in the store.

Shopping Goods *Shopping goods* are items selected after price and quality comparisons are made. Consumers usually spend more time, effort, and thought before making a buying decision on shopping goods. The two types of shopping goods are homogeneous and heterogeneous goods. *Homogeneous shopping goods* are viewed as being quite similar, with price being the primary purchase determinant. Many customers consider products such as eggs and milk to be homogeneous, where the best price rules the purchase decision. *Heterogeneous shopping goods* are viewed as unique, with quality or appropriateness for the application being the primary purchase determinant. Heterogeneous shopping goods include items such as furniture and gourmet foods. Salesperson assistance when purchasing homogeneous shopping goods is often limited, but for heterogeneous goods, the salesperson's role can be quite involved.

WORKSHOP

In a group, brainstorm to generate a list of products purchased by group members in the past month. Classify the products as impulse, convenience, shopping, or specialty goods.

Categories of Consumer Goods Related to Buying Habits

Impulse	Convenience	Shopping	Specialty
soft drinks	flour	small appliances	high-fashion items
magazines	sugar	television sets	cosmetics
candy bars	coffee	radios	watches
potato chips	bread	automobiles	motor oil
chewing gum	meat	furniture	sporting equipment
popcorn		clothing	

RETAIL SALES WITHOUT SALESPEOPLE Technology has made it possible for customers to complete a shopping transaction without any assistance from salespeople. Internet shopping, catalog shopping, and home shopping networks are examples of this. Sales kiosks have been installed in some retail stores, and shoppers can use these to pick out and purchase items they cannot find on store shelves but that might be in another store location or the warehouse. Some traditional stores even have added automated self-checkout stations so that customers can scan their own merchandise and pay with cash, check, or credit or debit card without any assistance from a cashier.

THINK CRITICALLY Do you think salespeople will ever be completely replaced by technology?

Specialty Goods *Specialty goods* are products about which consumers have knowledge, in which they have confidence, and for which they usually will not accept substitutes. A strong brand preference frequently is involved. Certain types of goods lend themselves to strong brand preference and are more often classified as specialty items. Examples of specialty goods are brand-name cosmetics and watches, high-fashion apparel, and sporting equipment. The buyer typically will go to a great deal of trouble to get the specialty item desired, and price usually is not a determining factor in the buying decision. The salesperson is expected to be knowledgeable and to provide specific assistance relating to issues such as quality and unique applications.

CHALLENGES OF RETAIL SELLING

Certain aspects of retail selling can create challenges. These challenges can be grouped into five categories: (1) image, (2) employee indifference, (3) peak-valley nature of demand, (4) working conditions, and (5) requirements of retail selling.

Image Traditionally, retail selling has not been considered a prestigious career. Many of the sales jobs that have contributed to this poor image have been eliminated by modern merchandising methods. Others are not career paths but are part-time or temporary employment held by individuals at the beginning or end of their careers. The career path of retail selling can lead to demanding, productive, and prestigious positions. Salespeople in these positions often are liberally rewarded with both money and satisfaction.

Employee Indifference Indifference by employees is evident in many forms. Examples of employee indifference include the following.

- A sales clerk who tells the customer that the store does not carry the brand he is looking for but does not offer to show the customer the brand the store does carry

- A salesperson who shows impatience with a customer who is trying to decide on a particular product

- Clerks visiting with each other rather than offering to assist customers

Experience indicates that 68 percent of customers who do not return to shop at a store say it is because of an indifferent attitude of a store employee.

6.1 BASICS OF RETAIL SELLING

A business cannot afford to employ salespeople with indifferent attitudes. Customers will not continue to patronize a store where employees are indifferent. Employees must be trained to show interest in customers and remember that the customer always comes first.

Peak-Valley Nature of Demand The *80-20 principle* emphasizes that 80 percent of the demand occurs during 20 percent of the time. This rule applies to the weekly schedule of a retail store as well as to the seasons of the year. It makes scheduling and employment of salespeople difficult.

Retail stores meet the demands of the peak times by hiring part-time salespeople. These employees usually are laid off after the peak seasons. This creates another challenge since these people often are not interested in the image of the business as they know they are there for just a short period of time. Also, there often is not a lot of time for training these employees.

Working Conditions Working conditions for in-store retail selling offer advantages and disadvantages. One advantage is that physical surroundings usually are pleasant. Another is that retail salespeople are in a position to contribute to the well-being of individuals who seek their help.

The amount of standing and moving around is considered a disadvantage by some, an advantage by others. The fact that retail salespeople have to work during hours or days when many other workers are off is a disadvantage to some, but others prefer being off while others are working.

Requirements of Retail Selling The most important requirement for the retail salesperson is product knowledge. Customers come to the store to see products and to get information about them. They look to the salesperson as their source of information. An individual who has been selling the same type of products for many years will have a great deal of knowledge about new products as well as information about previous products.

However, a newly hired salesperson or someone who is hired only for the peak season may have less knowledge than some customers who have used a particular brand of product for many years. Salespeople must take the time to study products so that they will be able to provide customers with the assistance they seek.

CHECKPOINT

Why do different types of goods require different levels of skill in selling?

KNOWING THE RETAIL CUSTOMER

In the retail industry, customer service plays an important role. The thing a customer will remember most is the service received. An effective salesperson will address the needs of customers first and then work to establish long-term customer relationships.

Customer relations depict how customers feel about the personnel, products, and services of a place of business. A business must treat each customer like she or he is the most important person ever to walk in the door of the business. Today, customers have more choices in the marketplace, are better educated, and are more willing to try new products and services than in the past. Salespeople play a large part in the decision of consumers to shop at particular retail establishments.

TYPES OF CUSTOMERS

Knowing the types of customers that visit a business will help the salespeople project a positive image for the company.

Decided customers know what they want to buy. You can identify decided customers by the way they walk, the look in their eyes, their tone of voice, and their facial expressions. They are positive in their movements. Decided customers like to make buying decisions.

Before they enter the store, decided customers often already know the item they want to buy. A friend may have recommended a certain product, or the customer already may have satisfactorily used the product or service. Perhaps the customer wants to buy a specific product because that customer shopped around and read all the available product information. Decided customers consider the merits of the product and are well informed before buying. Decided customers come into a store looking for a specific item. Usually these customers ask where the item is located. Decided customers often become irritated in a self-serve store or in a store where the salesperson is of little help. Because they know what they want to buy, they want immediate, friendly service.

Decided customers may ask a few questions about the product before making the purchase. Answer the questions that are asked. Give them the needed information. Let the customers do the talking. You may want to ask a question or two, but there is no need to give decided customers a complete sales presentation unless they request it. You should also be more knowledgeable about the item being purchased than your customers are.

Listen to your customers' opinions and what they have to say. Decided customers like salespeople who listen to them. Acting as if the customers are teaching you about the product helps build your customers' confidence. They may tell you something about the product that will be helpful in a future sales situation. Finally, never rush these customers into making an immediate decision. Decided customers do not like to be sold. After they have considered all the facts about the item, they want to make the final decision.

6.1 BASICS OF RETAIL SELLING

Undecided customers do not know what to buy. It is the salesperson's responsibility to help undecided customers make up their minds. Some undecided customers worry about making purchases, and it takes them a long time to decide. Salespeople easily can cause undecided customers to become confused about what to buy. You should show them only a few items. If you show them too much, they will become even more confused.

A common mistake some salespeople make is to continue to show more merchandise or give more information about too many products. These salespeople believe that they will eventually find a product that undecided customers will like, but they will only confuse these customers more. Rather than show undecided customers more merchandise, you should ask questions about their needs, the use of the product, and their likes and dislikes. Then you can better select one or two products you feel will satisfy their needs. By selecting one or two products and setting aside others they will not like, you will help undecided customers avoid further confusion and thus move closer to attaining the sale.

Make small, positive statements about the product, and don't ask questions. You should say, "The white shirt will look best for all occasions," rather than, "Do you like the blue shirt or the white one better?" Since it is difficult for undecided customers to make a choice, you may have to assume that they have made a decision. You should say, "We can deliver the home entertainment center tomorrow," rather than, "Would you like to have the home entertainment system delivered tomorrow?"

The **just-looking customer** may be a decided or undecided customer, but does not want the assistance of a salesperson. These are the most difficult customers to sell. These customers are hesitant to tell the salesperson what they are looking for, but they should not be ignored.

How often have you heard a salesperson ask, "May I help you?" and the customer answer, "No, I'm just looking"? When customers walk into a store, avoid saying, "May I help you?" Greet customers with a "hello" and a warm, friendly smile. Then pause and wait for a response. If they say they are just looking, ask if there is anything particular they are looking for. This may bring out a decided or undecided customer's desire for a particular product or service. The customer may say, "Where are shoes located?" or "I'm looking for an inexpensive birthday gift," or "I'm interested in a new set of golf clubs."

A just-looking customer may also be a *casual looker*. These customers really have nothing specific in mind to buy when they come into a store. They may not have been in the store for a long time and want to see what is new. Many people go shopping just to have something to do. Don't

133

ignore customers who tell you they are just looking. Invite them to look around your store. You may want to direct them to items of special interest or value. Make them feel welcome to shop in your store. Remember, customers who feel welcome will return to shop again. They may be casual lookers today and buyers tomorrow.

After you have invited customers to look around, don't forget them. Be alert. Don't get so involved in stock work and other duties that you forget your customers. Salespeople who offer assistance and then cannot be found when they are needed irritate customers.

If you see just-looking customers pause to look at an item, don't run over to them and begin a sales presentation. Customers who want to look around resent this. An alert salesperson carefully observes customers. If customers show an interest in an item by picking it up and looking around for a salesperson, you should then approach them and make a positive statement about the item. By talking about the merchandise, you probably can make a sale.

CUSTOMER MOODS

Customers can be classified as decided, undecided, or just-looking, but the mood of the customer can also be important. Customers' moods can change quickly based upon what they are buying, how they are being served, what their values are, and even what has happened to them earlier in the day. At one moment, customers may be friendly and decided, and at the next moment they may become impatient and dominating. You should be constantly alert to different customer moods. Advance preparation in handling different customer moods often results in a successful sale and a satisfied customer. Here are some suggestions for dealing with various customer moods.

Talkative When working with a talkative customer, try to direct the conversation to the merchandise. Do not allow the conversation to wander to other topics.

Silent Get the silent customer to talk by asking questions that require more than a "yes" or "no" response.

Friendly You can help the friendly customer by providing the information needed to make a wise buying decision. Talk "with" rather than "at" the customer.

Disagreeable or Argumentative Listen to, but do not argue with, this customer. Agree with minor points of the conversation and base your presentation upon these points of agreement.

Timid or Sensitive Be patient, and do not rush this customer. Use empathy to show support. Share factual information, and help the timid customer feel comfortable about purchasing the product or service.

Impatient Serve impatient customers promptly. Answer questions, but do not try to oversell. Speed up the sales presentation by giving only the basic features and customer benefits of the item being sold.

Dominating or Superior Let dominating or superior customers do the talking, and allow them to feel important. Present information quickly, and let these customers sell themselves.

Procrastinating These customers want to delay buying. Get them to agree to key selling points. After you have determined their needs, don't offer a choice. You may have to take the role of assuming they will buy.

6.1 BASICS OF RETAIL SELLING

CUSTOMER BUYING DECISIONS

Before a purchase is made, each person must have a need or want for a product or service. Based upon this need, the customer must answer five questions.

1. What product should I buy?
2. Where should I buy?
3. What price should I pay?
4. When should I buy?
5. What quantity should I buy?

No purchase is made until a customer has made all five decisions. All customers make these buying decisions, although they may not be aware of them. These decisions are based on the needs and wants of customers. When customers become consciously aware of a need, they make all five buying decisions and purchase a product or service to satisfy that need.

The Product to Buy The brand, price, convenience, reputation, size, model, color, quality, and style must all be considered when making a purchase. Today there are many similar kinds of products and services available to satisfy the different needs and wants of customers.

The Place to Buy Customers select a place to buy for various reasons, including service, salespeople, store atmosphere, and selection. For some customers, the place to buy is very important. The fact that a customer is proud to say a product or service was bought at a particular store reveals the importance of the store's image to the customer.

The Price to Pay Customers want to buy a product they feel is the best value for their money. The benefits of the product must be worth the price.

The Time to Buy Consumers must ask themselves how soon they need to make a purchase. Some purchases need to be made immediately, and others can wait. A customer who is just thinking about new clothes for the upcoming season can take her time in making a purchase, but an unexpected invitation to a party being held tomorrow can make the purchase of a new outfit an immediate need.

The Quantity to Buy Some products will be single-purpose items, and customers will buy only one. Items in this category include a camera, a television set, or a set of golf clubs. Some merchandise will require other products in order to function. A remote-controlled car will not function without batteries. A customer will have to decide how many batteries they want to purchase. Will one set be enough or will extras be required?

Why is it important for a salesperson to understand customers?

_____

_____

THINK CRITICALLY

1. How is retail selling different from other selling situations?

2. Briefly describe each of the four classifications of products.

3. Briefly describe the five challenges of retail selling.

4. Why is it important to know if a customer is a decided, undecided, or just-looking customer?

5. Why is it important to know the customer's mood?

6. What are the five decisions a customer must make before a purchase is made?

MAKE CONNECTIONS

7. **RESEARCH** Research careers in retail selling and determine a career path that leads to a high-level position in retail sales. Prepare a presentation of your findings for your class.

8. **COMMUNICATION** With a partner, role play selling situations with a decided, an undecided, and a just-looking customer.

9. **COMMUNICATION** Write a report summarizing how you were treated as a customer when making a recent purchase.

LESSON 6.2
SALES PROCESS IN RETAIL SELLING

GOALS

EXPLAIN the steps of Phase 1 of the sales process

ESTABLISH and **SOLVE** a problem for retail customers

EXPLAIN the importance of effective closing methods in retail selling

PHASE 1 OF THE SALES PROCESS

The sales process involves basic steps. In a retail setting, the same basic steps are followed, but the prospect comes to you and usually already has an interest in a particular product. Therefore, the sales process will be carried out somewhat differently.

PREPARING FOR PHASE 1

In preparation for Phase 1, you will prospect, size up prospects in the pre-approach, and prepare for customer objections. Then you are ready to begin the interview in Phase 1.

Prospecting Although prospecting in the retail store context is more limited than in any other type of selling, a substantial amount still can be done. The 80-20 principle suggests that the retail salesperson will have time to spend telephoning customers and preparing direct mail pieces.

ON THE $CENE

After Katie and James purchased several items for their new apartment at a local bed and bath shop, Josefina, their salesperson, sent them a thank you note along with a coupon for a 20 percent discount on their next purchase. Do you think this will encourage Katie and James to return there to shop?

An unexpected call or written message can generate interest from customers. Some examples of contacts a salesperson could make are as follows.

- "A beautiful, new, one-of-a-kind dress came in today, and I knew it would be perfect for you."

- "I hope you have received the coupons for our upcoming furniture sale. We have a new table that would fit perfectly with your great room furniture."

- "I know you've had your home entertainment system for three years now. This is a great time to think about upgrading. Can you come into the store this week?"

- "I remember that your twenty-fifth anniversary is next month. I wanted to congratulate you and let you know about a diamond ring your wife was looking at yesterday."

Receiving messages like these will make a customer feel comfortable coming into the store and asking for you. The customer will feel like you are expecting him or her

Pre-approach In retail selling, pre-approach activities are largely limited to sizing up the prospect to the greatest extent possible before the approach. Learning customers' names and keeping appropriate records also help. As limited as these activities are, they may provide an advantage in the approach phase. In addition, when two or more persons come to the store together, it often is possible to get information discreetly from one person about the other.

When a customer enters a store, the salesperson should stop all other activities, such as personal conversation, stock work, paperwork, and housekeeping duties, and should observe the customer's manner. This can help the salesperson determine if the customer is hurried or relaxed and ascertain the customer's mood.

Handling Objections Objections can come at any phase of the sales interview, and the salesperson must be prepared to handle them whenever they are raised. Objections play a more important role in the development of the interview in retail sales than in other sales situations. The scene is less leisurely—both parties are likely to be standing, and other customers are probably waiting for help. As a result, the dialogue is more direct. Getting the prospect to state objections quickly is a way of getting down to business. The steps for handling objections that were discussed in Chapter 4 can be applied to the retail sales process.

6.2 SALES PROCESS IN RETAIL SELLING

GAINING THE INTERVIEW

The initial phase of the sales interview consists of things said and done between the time the first contact is made and the time the second phase, establishing the problem, begins. The steps that lead to the *interview* are very important in a retail setting. The steps in the first phase of the retail sale are the acknowledgment, the greeting, and the approach.

The Acknowledgment In retail sales, the customer initiates the interview by moving into the presence of a salesperson or into some other position in which she or he can reasonably expect to be seen and greeted. The **acknowledgment** occurs when the salesperson has seen and greeted the customer. The customer wants to feel welcome, and a simple friendly acknowledgment by the salesperson helps to achieve this feeling. If the salesperson is busy and no one else is available to offer assistance, a nod and a smile will acknowledge the presence of the customer.

The Greeting Statements made when the salesperson first speaks to the customer are referred to as the **greeting**. The salesperson who is not busy should offer a smile and a greeting such as "Good morning," "Welcome," "Welcome—come in," or "Hello." The acknowledgment and the greeting are two different aspects of the approach, even though most of the time they occur together. They are separated by a time interval in the following two circumstances.

1. When it is necessary to finish with the current customer
2. When the new customer indicates a desire to be left alone for a time to look at the merchandise

Because your attitude toward the customer is very important, the actual words spoken are really not that important. Your attitude toward the customer should incorporate the following thoughts.

- The customer is your reason for being there
- Customers help pay your salary
- Customers come to you for help
- Your training and knowledge of the store's merchandise puts you in a unique position to help others
- You are glad you are in the business of dealing with people rather than with things

The Approach In many interviews, no approach is needed because the customer immediately starts describing what she or he wants. If the approach is used, the proper choice of words is important. The words used depend on on whether the service approach or the amenities approach is used.

The **service approach** is a method of greeting the customer by questioning to determine if service is needed. Examples are

- "May I help you?"
- "May I serve you?"
- "May I be of assistance?"
- "Is someone helping you?"

In a group, describe your shopping experiences and the best and worst interview approaches you have seen a retail salesperson use.

139

Most experts in retail selling do not like this approach because it can make customers feel as though they are being rushed. Another reason not to use the service approach is that it may force customers to take a position on their degree of readiness to buy before they are prepared to make such a commitment. When a customer is confronted with, "May I help you?" the reply is usually negative. This reply is often followed by the prospect's departure.

Another problem with the service approach is that it leads salespeople to be less alert when handling customers. Salespeople become accustomed to asking a customer, "May I help you?" and forget about the steps of acknowledging and greeting the customer.

The **amenities approach** starts the conversation on a personal basis with comments from the salesperson that are pleasant and thoughtful and that show an interested tone that characterizes social exchanges. The customer is singled out as the distinct individual that she or he is. Using the amenities approach, the relationship can be established in just a few seconds after the greeting with a remark like one of the following.

- "What a beautiful blouse!"
- "Is it still cold outside?"
- "What a beautiful baby!"
- "I see you go to The University of Georgia. How do you like it?"

The customer's reply will tell the salesperson whether to continue the personal talk or get right down to business. Either way, the customer senses that his or her individuality has been recognized. Sometimes common interests make it possible to develop a bond in a short time. The amenities approach often elicits personal information that proves helpful later in the interview.

One version of the amenities approach is referred to as the merchandise approach. The *merchandise approach* is a method in which the salesperson departs after the customer has indicated a desire to be left alone for awhile but returns when the customer seems to be interested in a particular item. Some comments the salesperson might use include

- "Isn't that nice? It's our newest line."
- "That's been very popular."
- "Isn't it comfortable? And it packs for travel so nicely."
- "It has a two-year warranty."

This approach minimizes the chance of scaring away the unsure customer and gets the sale going in a comfortable manner.

What is the purpose of Phase 1 of the sales process?

6.2 SALES PROCESS IN RETAIL SELLING

PHASE 2 OF THE SALES PROCESS

In Phase 2 of the sales process, your goal will be to establish the problem or need of the customer and then solve the problem.

ESTABLISHING THE PROBLEM OR NEED

The key to the sale is establishing the customer's problem or need. Ability to do that comes from listening to the customer and asking questions to fill in gaps. It is helpful for the retail salesperson to determine, as soon as possible, the degree to which the customer is aware of the specific product wanted. For the *decided customer,* all the store needs to do is have the product the customer is seeking available, agree on terms, establish confidence in the store and the salesperson, and finalize the sale by getting the customer to make a decision to buy now.

The salesperson can make a real contribution to the *undecided customer* and the *just-looking customer.* Information provided by the customer is most useful in helping the salesperson determine which product will satisfy the customer's needs. Questions asked of the customer should be kept to a minimum, especially at first. The customer may not know the specific answer but may make something up to avoid feeling foolish. Such incorrect information puts the salesperson on the wrong track. Furthermore, asking too many questions may give customers the impression that the salesperson wants to sell them something as soon as possible and get them out of the store. Whenever possible, neutral probes, such as silence, encouragement, and elaboration, should be used instead of questions.

In the retail sales process, establishing the problem and solving the problem are handled at the same time.

SOLVING THE PROBLEM

Presenting and demonstrating the product are principal methods of finding solutions to the customer's problem. During this presentation and demonstration, the salesperson should explain the product's features and describe its benefits. When solving the problem in retail sales, it is especially wise to first decide what to show and then decide how to show it.

What to Show When the interview moves to the stage of showing products, the salesperson must decide what to show first. Choosing this item can be crucial when the customer is unsure whether to buy now or to wait.

An off-target selection could end the interview. The salesperson's success at this stage will depend on the salesperson's judgment and the quality of the input received from the customer.

How to Show The customer tends to react to a product as the salesperson does. Therefore, the salesperson must feel and show excitement about the product. Salespeople should not put on false enthusiasm when showing a product but should gain enthusiasm and satisfaction from pleasing the customer. The customer should be actively involved in the showing of the product. Keeping the customer involved will increase customer interest in and create desire for the product or service, help the customer develop a sense of ownership, and get the customer to offer more information to determine additional needs and wants.

Use the Five Senses People use the five senses of touch, smell, taste, sight, and hearing to gather information about things around them. A successful salesperson will attempt to appeal to as many of these senses as possible during a sales presentation. The purpose of this appeal is to familiarize the customer with the product and to develop a sense of ownership. For example, makeup can be experienced through the senses of sight, touch, and smell. A customer may think a pair of boots looks great, and if buying the boots satisfies a fashion need, then the sight of the boots is enough to develop a sense of ownership. However, if the customer has a need for a pair of boots that is comfortable, just looking at the boots probably will not satisfy this need for comfort. The customer will want to try the boots on to experience the comfort. Trying on the boots will give the customer the opportunity to decide if the product will satisfy this need for comfort.

Start with the Product To understand how to appeal to your customer's senses, you must start with the product. Determine how many ways the customer can experience the product. Clothing can be experienced through sight and touch. Clothing being purchased for personal use should

6.2 SALES PROCESS IN RETAIL SELLING

MEETING NEEDS OF MINORITY GROUPS

Retail establishments are offering merchandise and information in other languages to meet the needs of growing ethnic populations. In many communities, these activities are targeted toward Hispanics, the fastest-growing ethnic minority in the United States. The population grew about 60 percent between 1999 and 2000 while the United States population as a whole grew 13 percent according to 2000 census data.

Many Home Depot stores now have signs on their aisle markers in both English and Spanish. Gateway computers recently conducted a massive advertising project targeting the Hispanic population with Spanish-language advertising and computers equipped with Spanish-language software and keyboards. Gateway has also added Spanish-speaking customer support representatives and sales clerks. Other stores in areas with a large Hispanic population feature Latino music and have special merchandise, such as books, printed in Spanish.

THINK CRITICALLY Why is it important for stores to offer services and merchandise in a language other than English?

---

be tried on and viewed in a mirror. A CD player can be experienced through the sense of hearing. By listening to the sound of the player, your customer can experience and judge the quality of the product.

Handle the Product Carefully As a salesperson, remember that while you are watching and observing the customer, the customer is also observing you. The customer will notice how you handle the merchandise. The product, regardless of its price, deserves the respect of the salesperson. If you handle it roughly and carelessly, it gives the customer the impression that the product is not very valuable. On the other hand, if you handle the product with care, the customer will see the product as a valuable investment.

Always handle the product so that the customer can see the product and the features you are trying to highlight. Small items should be brought as close as possible for the customer to see. A salesperson's hands should not cover important features of the product. With larger products, the salesperson should make sure that the customer is following the sales demonstration by pointing clearly to the product features being discussed. Improper handling of the product by the salesperson could result in the loss of a sale.

Describe how problems are established and solved.

PHASE 3 OF THE SALES PROCESS

Closing the sale is generally easier in retailing than in other types of selling because more retail sales are made in a given time period. One reason for this is that the timing of the need to buy and contact with the salesperson is usually closer. Another is that the prospect normally comes to the salesperson seeking a product or service. This lessens the problem of the salesperson appearing to be dominant over the customer.

Retail sales generally have a lower commission rate than other types of sales where other phases of the sales process are stronger determinants of success than closing. Therefore, it is important for retail salespeople to develop good closing skills. All of the material on closing in Chapter 5 also relates to retail selling. The indirect closing method, which involves proceeding with details of the purchase on the assumption the buying decision has been made, is particularly useful. Examples of this method are

- "Mr. Russell, what is your full name?"
- "Where would you like delivery made?"
- "Will this be cash or charge?"
- "Would you like this gift wrapped?"
- "We deliver in your area on Friday. Would that be satisfactory?"
- "Will you take this with you or should we deliver it?"
- "Now let's see what will go well with it."

When the system requires turning the customer over to a cashier, if store traffic permits, it is a good idea to stay with the customer until the sale is completed and payment is made. After each sales contact, when there is time, it is a good business practice to present a sales card with a sincere invitation for a return visit and a request to tell others about your business. Regardless of whether a sale was made, the customer should leave the store with the feeling that the visit was appreciated and that a return trip is anticipated.

CHECKPOINT

Describe the importance of good closing skills.

6.2 SALES PROCESS IN RETAIL SELLING

THINK CRITICALLY

1. What are some ways a salesperson can prospect for retail sales?

2. How can a salesperson learn about a prospect in a retail setting?

3. Distinguish between the acknowledgment, the greeting, and the approach in a retail sales situation.

4. What is the best way to establish a customer's problem or need?

5. Why is it important to appeal to as many of the customer's senses as possible when showing a product?

6. Which closing method has been found to be the most useful in retail selling?

MAKE CONNECTIONS

7. **RESEARCH** Interview a retail salesperson. Find out what techniques are used in the sales process by the salesperson. Present your findings to your class.

8. **COMMUNICATION** With a partner, role play a selling situation that could take place in your favorite store using the amenities approach.

9. **RESEARCH** Search the Internet for information on trends in retail selling. Prepare a report or a display on the information you find.

145

LESSON 6.3
OTHER SKILLS FOR RETAIL SELLING

REALIZE the importance of activities after the sale

EXPLAIN the importance of handling common situations correctly

UNDERSTAND the importance of accurate sales records

AFTER THE SALE

Activities after the sale are an important part of the sales process. Some of the follow-up activities can take place in the store before the customer leaves with the merchandise. Other follow-up activities will be conducted after the sale is complete in order to encourage the customer to return to the store to make additional purchases.

SUGGESTIVE SELLING

Suggestive selling can be described as the face-to-face effort to motivate the customer to buy more now and, if done correctly, to buy more often. Suggestive selling is one of the best ways a salesperson can increase sales. What the salesperson is really doing is suggesting complementary items that will *round out* the order.

ON THE $CENE

Katie and James had selected a rug for the living room in their apartment. That was all they planned to purchase on their trip to the store, but the salesperson showed them some sofa pillows and other accessories that would look great with the rug. They couldn't resist purchasing the items the salesperson suggested. Do you like for a salesperson to suggest other items to go along with something you are purchasing?

6.3 OTHER SKILLS FOR RETAIL SELLING

Suggestive selling may be used to start a sale, while demonstrating a product, or at the end of a sale. Displaying and/or demonstrating related items together helps the customer visualize the functions or qualities of the merchandise and assists in suggestive selling. Suggestions can also be made by using promotional cards or letters and by making telephone calls to inform customers of items in other areas or departments of the store. Suggestions should be positive and should explain the merchandise and relate it to the customer or to other merchandise.

The types of merchandise that can be suggested include compatible merchandise, fashionable merchandise, and promotional or stand merchandise.

Compatible merchandise Related or accessory items that enhance, accentuate, or can be used with other merchandise are compatible merchandise. Showing the customer jewelry that was made to enhance a new outfit would be an example of this.

Fashionable merchandise Newest or latest styles, fads, bestsellers, and quality merchandise are fashionable merchandise. An example of this would be showing a customer a new style of shoe when the customer comes in looking for shoes just like the shoes she is wearing.

Promotional or stand merchandise Items marked down, special-price or value items, larger quantities, or seasonal merchandise are promotional or stand merchandise. A special handbag that can be purchased if a customer buys a certain brand of clothing would be an example of promotional merchandise.

MAINTAIN CUSTOMER CONTACT

Once the sale is complete, you should maintain contact with your customer. The follow-up methods that were discussed in Chapters 2 and 5 can be applied in a retail setting. Other techniques used to maintain contact with customers include the following.

- **Mailing List** Many retail stores have their customers join a mailing list to receive special notices for upcoming sales and special offers.

- **Customer Loyalty Plans** These plans encourage customers to return to a particular store by awarding the customer points or credits toward future purchases for all items purchased at the store.

- **Birthday Offers** Special birthday gifts or discounts are also offered to customers to encourage them to come in and shop.

Why are activities conducted after the sale important to the sales process?

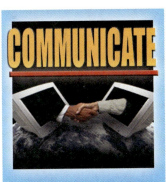

COMMUNICATE

You are selling clothes in the children's department at a local store. A young mother comes in looking for a dress for her daughter. Make a list of items you will suggest to go with the dress she picks out. Practice making these suggestions to a partner.

147

COMMON SITUATIONS IN RETAIL SELLING

The daily activities of the retail salesperson involve a number of situations and routines, including handling more than one customer, group shopping, the turnover, substitution, and exchanges, returned goods, and complaints.

HANDLING MORE THAN ONE CUSTOMER

It usually is better for a customer to have the exclusive attention of the salesperson. This is not always possible, and there will be times when you must wait on more than one customer at a time. During peak traffic periods or when a customer is taking a long time to make a decision, it may be the only way to achieve satisfaction for everyone. Another situation that can arise is when a customer comes in while you are waiting on someone else but lets you know that it will only take a few moments to handle the customer's need.

The salesperson should get permission from the current customer before going to help others. You could use a statement like, "Would you mind if I check with the customer over there for a moment? I'll be right back." Usually, the current customer will not object to being left for a short time and may even appreciate having more time in which to reach a buying decision. However, a sale that is being finalized should not be interrupted.

GROUP SHOPPING

It is not unusual for more than one person to be involved in a buying decision, and sometimes a customer will bring helpers along. In most cases, this makes for a more difficult sale because of group behavior patterns that develop, such as problems reaching consensus and peer pressure within the group. In some instances, the sale becomes easier because the customer may follow expected behavior patterns rather than more individualistic responses.

The key to handling groups is to use neutral probes and comments until a consensus appears to be emerging. The salesperson should be cautious about deciding who the dominant individual is and siding with that person early in the interview. This could lead to alienation of others who might not like their peer's attempt at dominance. The domineering person will sometimes even resent the implication that help is needed from a salesperson.

THE TURNOVER

In retail sales, the *turnover* describes a situation in which the salesperson turns the customer over to someone else in an effort to close the sale. Many retail stores use such a routine. The turnover is justified in three situations.

1. When the salesperson recognizes that he or she is not qualified to handle the customer's needs. Newer salespeople or those lacking certain specialized training can take care of most problems, but not all.

2. When the customer seems to be unhappy with the salesperson, perhaps because of a difference in age, gender, dialect, taste, or personality.

3. When the salesperson is unable to satisfy the customer. This happens more often in problem-resolution situations than in need-satisfying ones.

6.3 OTHER SKILLS FOR RETAIL SELLING

The second salesperson usually is introduced as a buyer or as a specialist. The salesperson who is not a buyer can appropriately be referred to as a specialist. Such titles add prestige, which gives the customer the confidence needed in the situation. Many stores give bonuses to both salespeople to encourage the use of the turnover in retail selling.

SUBSTITUTION

When a salesperson tries to get a customer to buy something other than what was requested, the attempt is referred to as *substitution*. The substitution may involve brands (Nike instead of Adidas), product lines (running shoes instead of tennis shoes), or price lines. Substituting a higher-priced line is known as *trading up* and may involve the other types of substitution mentioned.

A question of ethics is raised when substitution works to the disadvantage of the customer. Professional salespeople will not use substitution in this way, and those who do are not likely to be in the selling business for long. The biggest problem here is determining whether the substitution is an advantage or a disadvantage to the customer. Making this determination is complicated by the subjective nature of consumer satisfaction. Probably the best time to use the substitution practice is when it increases the consumer's choices.

Making substitutions requires no more than the basic selling skills. Product knowledge is very important because the substitution should be limited primarily to comparing the two products on the basis of facts, features, and benefits. When the attempt involves substituting one product for a requested item that is not in stock, this comparison is all the more important to convince the customer that the items really are interchangeable.

The product requested should not be downgraded. Salespeople should avoid the following commonly used statements, not only because they downgrade products but also because they may even violate sales law.

- ■ "We don't stock that product because it is inferior."
- ■ "We don't stock that anymore because we had so much trouble with it."
- ■ "This is just as good."
- ■ "This is better."
- ■ "They've just about quit making that."
- ■ "There is no such product. You must be thinking of. . . ."

Such statements can offend the prospect and tend to build resistance toward substitution. The salesperson might instead say, "That might well serve your needs, but you may want to consider this product before you decide."

EXCHANGES, RETURNED GOODS, AND COMPLAINTS

The salesperson in a retail store must deal daily with goods being returned for cash or credit or exchanged for other goods. Stores will have policies about returns and exchanges that must be followed. These policies should be posted in the store so that customers are aware of them when making purchases. If the customer is not pleased with what you can offer according to store policy, you should ask a manager for assistance.

Complaints, with requests for adjustments or repairs, are frequent. Even where special departments handle complaints, the customer usually will come back to the salesperson first. A friendly, personal greeting will sometimes calm an emotional customer. When it does not, you must use self-control to avoid becoming upset. Remember the customer just needs help. The customer's problem should be established using neutral probes of silence, encouragement, and elaboration. Letting the customer verbally express anger defuses emotion, and verbalizing the complaint puts it into perspective. After agreement has been reached about the problem, the next steps are to find a solution and to get the customer to accept it. Everything should be done to satisfy the problem within the bounds of what is reasonable and within company rules.

CHECKPOINT

Why is it important for a salesperson to know how to deal with situations such as handling more than one customer and group shopping?

_____
_____

SHOW ME THE MONEY

Sales records are important and should be kept accurately and in a timely manner. These records are used to record sales transactions and complete financial statements and help the accounting department determine the amount of sales tax and income tax the company owes to the government.

SALES RECEIPTS

A **sales receipt** is a written record of a sale. Sales receipts are often referred to as sales slips, sales checks, or sales forms. These receipts are important to a business because they serve as the customer's record of the sale and as a vital source of information for the business.

Most businesses now use computerized cash registers that are equipped with a bar code reader. The cashier or sales clerk scans the bar code on the product in front of the bar code reader. The bar code reader sends the information to the store's computer system, and a description of the item being purchased is printed on the receipt. When the sale is complete, the cashier or clerk enters the method of payment, and a receipt is printed.

6.3 OTHER SKILLS FOR RETAIL SELLING

All sales registers start the business day with an opening change fund. As sales are made during the day, the amount of money in the sales register drawer increases. At the end of the day's activities, the total amount of cash received is printed automatically on the sales register tape. The total amount of cash in the drawer, plus any cash paid out, plus the checks and credit cards sales, minus the opening change fund should equal the total amount printed on the sales register tape. This is called *proving cash*. If the cash received is equal to the cash received on the sales register tape, cash proves. If the cash received is less than the cash received on the sales register tape, cash is short. If the cash received is more than the cash received on the sales register tape, cash is over.

Gena's cash drawer started the day with $45.00 in the opening change fund and at the end of the day had $250.52 in cash, $48.00 in checks, and $30.95 in credit card sales. She paid out $16.50 for a return, and cash sales for the day were $300.97. Does cash prove in Gena's drawer?

SOLUTION

Add the cash, checks, and credit card sales together.

$250.52 + $48.00 + $30.95 = $329.47

Add receipts for cash paid out during the day.

$329.47 + $16.50 = $345.97

Subtract the amount of the opening change fund to find the cash received.

$345.97 − $45.00 = $300.97

Compare the cash received with the total of cash sales for the day.

$300.97 = $300.97

Cash proves in Gena's drawer.

SALES RETURNS AND EXCHANGES

Sometimes customers return merchandise for cash refunds or credit to their charge accounts or in exchange for other merchandise. When merchandise is exchanged for other merchandise that is less expensive, the customer must be refunded the difference plus the tax charged on the difference. If the customer originally paid with a credit card, the difference can be credited to the account. Receipts are prepared to document these transactions.

PAYING FOR MERCHANDISE

Customers may pay for merchandise in a variety of ways. Some customers will use cash while others will write a check or use a credit card or debit card. The method for handling the transaction will vary according to the method of payment being made.

Cash If the customer is paying with cash, the money presented to the cashier or clerk should be counted very carefully, and the amount received should be entered on the keypad of the cash register. The computerized cash register will calculate the amount of change that is due to the customer. The cashier or clerk is then responsible for counting the required amount of change and giving it to the customer. The change should be recounted as it is presented to the customer.

Checks If the customer is paying by check, be sure to follow company policy on check acceptance. Most businesses will accept a check only for the amount of the purchase. There may be a limit on the amount for which a personal check can be written. Check to be sure that the customer has made the check payable to your company, filled in the correct amount on the check in written and numerical format, used the present date, and signed the check. Some electronic sales registers will even fill in the check for the customer in order to prevent errors. Many businesses require photo identification, such as a driver's license, and one other form of identification to verify the customer's identity. Be sure to write on the check all required information from the identification. All of this information must be written on the front of the check in the borders. The back of the check is used only for endorsements.

The company you work for will have policies regarding out-of-state checks, payroll checks, traveler's checks, or government checks. Always follow company policies regarding checks.

Credit Cards When a customer presents a credit card, the card is swiped through the electronic card reader. The amount of the sale and the account number are recorded in the computer's memory and on the cash register tape. The cash register prints a receipt for the customer to sign and leave with the cashier or clerk and a receipt for the customer to take. At the end of the day, credit and debit card sales are transmitted electronically to the company that processes these sales for the business.

When accepting a credit card for payment on a purchase, the salesperson should verify that the person presenting the credit card is a person authorized to use the card by checking the customer's identification on a driver's license or other photo identification and by comparing the signature on the back of the credit card with the customer's signature on the credit card sales form. If you notice a discrepancy, immediately notify your supervisor or follow the standard procedures outlined by your business.

Debit Cards Customers sometimes may use a debit card to make a purchase. A debit card looks like a credit card, but the amount of the sale is automatically deducted from the customer's checking or savings account. A debit card is sometimes referred to as a checking card or banking card.

When accepting a debit card for payment of merchandise, the salesperson should ask for identification before asking the customer to slide the debit card through the automated card reader. This ensures that the person using the card is the card's owner.

WORKSHOP

In a group, brainstorm to produce a list of policies used by stores regarding returns and exchanges and check, credit card, and debit card acceptance. Discuss why you think the stores have these policies.

Explain the importance of keeping accurate records of sales transactions.

6.3 OTHER SKILLS FOR RETAIL SELLING

THINK CRITICALLY

1. What is the purpose of suggestive selling?
   _____
   _____
   _____

2. Why is contact with customers after the sale important?
   _____
   _____
   _____

3. What are some common situations that retail salespeople should know how to handle?
   _____
   _____
   _____
   _____

4. When a customer pays for merchandise with a check, what steps must you follow?
   _____
   _____
   _____
   _____

5. When a customer pays for merchandise with a credit card, what steps must you follow?
   _____
   _____
   _____
   _____

MAKE CONNECTIONS

6. **COMMUNICATION** Use the table format in your word processing software. In the first column, make a list of items sold in your favorite store. In the second, third, and fourth columns, list items that could be sold along with the first item if suggestive selling was being used.

7. **BUSINESS MATH** Rhonda works as a sales clerk at a retail clothing store. At the end of the day, she must prove her cash drawer. Rhonda had the following money in her drawer. Is Rhonda's cash proved, cash over, or cash short?

Change	$ 12.65
Bills	270.00
Checks	132.45
Credit Card Sales	47.90
Cash Paid Out	30.00
Opening Change Fund	65.00
Cash Received on Sales Register Tape	424.60

153

REVIEW

CHAPTER SUMMARY

LESSON 6.1 Basics of Retail Selling
A. Retail selling is different from other selling situations because the customer comes to you with an interest in buying. Types of goods sold in retail stores include impulse, convenience, shopping, and specialty goods.

B. Customers enter a retail transaction as a decided customer, undecided customer, or just-looking customer. You will help them go through the steps of the buying decision based on the type of customer they are.

LESSON 6.2 Sales Process in Retail Selling
A. Prospecting and the pre-approach can be conducted in retail selling, but they are not as extensive as in other types of selling. In Phase 1, customers should be acknowledged, greeted, and approached.

B. In Phase 2, the problem must be established and solved. Determining what to show and how to show it are part of the problem-solving process.

C. Phase 3 closes the sale. The indirect closing method is often used in retail selling.

LESSON 6.3 Other Skills for Retail Selling
A. After the sale, the salesperson can offer other items by using suggestive selling. It is also important for the salesperson to maintain contact with customers after the sale.

B. There are many times when a salesperson will have to wait on more than one customer at a time or deal with group shopping. Sometimes you will not be able to help a customer and will need to turn him over to another salesperson.

C. Sales records are very important to a business. It is important that sales receipts, cash, checks, credit cards, and debit cards always be handled according to company policy.

VOCABULARY BUILDER

Choose the term that best fits the definition. Write the letter of the answer in the space provided. Some terms may not be used.

____ 1. Know what they want to buy

____ 2. Do not know what to buy

____ 3. May or may not know what they want to buy but do not want the assistance of a salesperson

____ 4. Occurs when the salesperson has seen and greeted the customer

____ 5. Questions the customer to determine if service is needed

____ 6. Starts the conversation on a personal basis

____ 7. Face-to-face effort to motivate the customer to buy more now

____ 8. Written record of a sale

a. acknowledgment
b. amenities approach
c. decided customers
d. greeting
e. just-looking customer
f. sales receipt
g. service approach
h. suggestive selling
i. undecided customers

CHAPTER 6

REVIEW CONCEPTS

9. Why is understanding the 80-20 principle so important in retail sales?
   _____
   _____

10. Which classification of product requires the most effort from the salesperson? Why?
    _____
    _____
    _____

11. Why is a salesperson concerned with customer relations?
    _____
    _____
    _____

12. How can you identify a decided customer?
    _____
    _____
    _____

13. What factors help the customer determine what to buy and where to buy it?
    _____
    _____
    _____

14. What can the salesperson do to prepare for Phase 1 of retail selling?
    _____
    _____

15. When can the greeting and acknowledgment be separated by a short period of time?
    _____
    _____
    _____

16. What are the differences in the service approach and the amenities approach?
    _____
    _____
    _____

17. What should the salesperson remember when showing a product?
_____
_____

18. How should a customer feel when leaving a store?
_____
_____

19. In suggestive selling, what types of merchandise can be suggested?
_____
_____
_____

20. Why must all transactions involving the sale, return, or exchange of merchandise be recorded in the sales register?
_____
_____

21. Why does a business accept different forms of payment for merchandise?
_____
_____

APPLY WHAT YOU LEARNED

22. Describe how a specific stereo system could be an impulse good to one customer, a convenience good to another, a shopping good to another, and a specialty good to yet another.
_____
_____
_____
_____

23. As a salesperson, which of the challenges described in Lesson 6.1 do you think would be the most difficult for you to deal with? Why?
_____
_____

24. Do you think there are any sales situations when the service approach would work better than the amenities approach? Explain your answer.
_____
_____

CHAPTER 6

25. You are working as a salesperson in a hardware store. All salespeople enter their own sales into the sales register, take payments, and give customers receipts. You have noticed that one of your coworkers, Kris, does not enter all transactions into the sales register. When one of her friends comes in, Kris will put money into the register without entering any sales information. You have also seen her record a very expensive item as something less expensive and not collect the correct amount of money from the customer. What would you do?

_____

_____

26. You have recently started working in an outdoor store. You always have enjoyed hiking and camping and are looking forward to learning more about the equipment the store carries. A man comes into the store who says he has been a Boy Scout leader for more than 20 years. He starts questioning you about a tent that is on display. You do not feel qualified to answer his questions. What would you do?

_____

_____

MAKE CONNECTIONS

27. **RESEARCH** When working in sales, you may have a customer who tries to give you counterfeit currency. Search the Internet for information on currency and prepare a report that could be given to salespeople to help them spot counterfeit currency.

28. **PROBLEM SOLVING** A customer came into your store today with a blouse she wanted to return. There were no tags on the blouse, and she did not have a sales receipt. You recognize the blouse as an item you sold more than six months ago. The blouse was put on clearance about three months ago. The customer insists that she purchased the blouse for full price and is demanding a full refund. What would you do? Write your solution to the problem.

29. **BUSINESS MATH** Use a spreadsheet to calculate the cash proof for Avery's register drawer. Avery had the following money in her drawer. Is Avery's cash proved, cash over, or cash short?

Change	$ 17.65
Bills	279.00
Checks	216.50
Credit Card Sales	75.30
Cash Paid Out	25.00
Opening Change Fund	200.00
Cash Received on Sales Register Tape	426.20

30. **COMMUNICATION** Research the customer service policy of a retail store in your area or of a national chain. Prepare a presentation on the information you find and present it to your class.

GLOSSARY

A

Acknowledgment occurs when the salesperson has seen and greeted the customer (p. 139)

Amenities approach starts the conversation on a personal basis with comments from the salesperson that are pleasant and thoughtful and that show an interested tone that characterizes social exchanges (p.140)

Attributes personality characteristics that contribute to the success of a salesperson (p. 9)

B

Benefits the advantages that could result from features (p. 48)

Blind search a random attempt to find and identify potential customers (p. 59)

C

Canned presentation directed at satisfying the needs of the majority of the customers who could use the product (p. 81)

Closing the customer accepts the product or service you are selling and purchases it (p. 98)

Contracts agreements, binding by law, that determine the rights and duties of the contracting parties (p. 102)

Convenience goods items bought from the most convenient, acceptable retail outlet (p. 129)

Customized presentation based on the specific needs and requirements of the prospect (p. 81)

D

Data mining the process of using automation to detect relevant patterns in a database (p. 29)

Decided customers prospects who know what they want to buy (p. 132)

Direct request closing method that involves a request for the prospect to place the order immediately (p. 109)

E

Empathy the ability to understand the situation from the other person's perspective (p. 10)

F

FAQs questions about a product that are commonly asked by customers (p. 40)

Features physical characteristics or capabilities of a product or service (p. 48)

Fulfillment the delivery of merchandise promptly, accurately, and in good condition (p. 37)

G

General benefit strategy tells customers who you are, whom you represent, what you do, and what you can do for them (p. 55)

Greeting statements made when the salesperson first speaks to the customer (p. 139)

Guarantee a promise about the quality of the product or service (p. 56)

I

Imagination the ability to apply creativity to a specific situation (p. 11)

Impending event closing method that involves stressing to the prospect that the decision to buy should be made now because something may happen soon that will make a delay costly (p. 109)

Impulse goods items bought in haste, with little or no thought as to the wisdom of the purchase (p. 129)

Indirect request closing method that involves behavior by the salesperson based on the assumption that the prospect has decided to buy (p. 109)

Industry a particular group of businesses with similar products (p. 56)

Integrity the ability to distinguish between right and wrong and to make decisions based on that distinction (p. 10)

Internet a network of public networks available almost anywhere (p. 32)

Interpersonal skills those skills that help you work well with others (p. 12)

Intranet an internal network used by a select group, such as employees of a company (p. 32)

J

Just-looking customers prospects who may be decided or undecided, but do not want the assistance of a salesperson (p.133)

K

Key-point presentation lists major points of the product and gives all the reasons for purchasing it (p. 81)

GLOSSARY

L
Lead qualification determines whether or not a prospect has three things—a recognized need, buying power, and receptivity and accessibility (p. 72)

M
Manufacturing salesperson person who sells products to other manufacturers or directly to wholesalers or retailers (p. 6)

Maslow's Hierarchy of Needs model that arranges needs in ascending order of importance: physiological needs, safety or security needs, social needs, esteem needs, and self-actualization needs (p. 49)

Monopoly exclusive control over a commercial activity (p. 104)

N
Narrowing the choice closing method that repeats the part of the process when alternatives are considered (p. 110)

Needs assessment interviewing the customer to determine his or her specific needs and wants and the range of options the customer has for satisfying them (p. 78)

O
Objection any type of sales resistance by the prospect (p. 85)

P
Patience the ability to keep your emotions out of the sales process in order to make the sale and benefit the client (p. 11)

Persistence unwillingness to take no for an answer (p. 9)

Personal selling direct communication between a sales representative and one or more prospective buyers who attempt to influence each other in a purchase situation (p. 48)

Pre-approach the initial contact with a prospect (p. 72)

Probing an attempt by the salesperson to gain additional sales-related information from the prospect (p. 79)

Prospecting the process of searching for individuals who qualify as potential customers for the product or service you are selling (p. 59)

R
Relationship selling emphasizes the relationship between a salesperson and buyer (p. 51)

Repeat business a customer returns to your business for a subsequent purchase (p. 39)

Repeat customer a person who returns to shop at a certain business (p. 5)

Retail sales a salesperson sells merchandise and services to a consumer (p. 6)

S
Sales automation technology that helps salespeople better manage important account information (p. 28)

Sales presentation the part of the sales process when the salesperson explains how a product or service will benefit the customer (p. 15)

Sales proposal written document used to offer a product or service to a client (p. 18)

Sales receipt a written record of a sale (p. 150)

Screeners individuals who answer calls for the prospects you are trying to contact (p. 73)

Securities, commodities, and financial service representatives people who work with institutions and individuals who want to invest money (p. 6)

Selective search any prospecting method that is not random (p. 60)

Self-motivation the ability to control your own activities (p. 11)

Selling process of explaining how a product or service will benefit your customers and meet their needs; involves the art of communicating effectively with people (p. 5)

Service approach method of greeting the customer by questioning to determine if service is needed (p. 139)

Shopping goods items selected after price and quality comparisons are made (p. 129)

Special offer closing method that involves offering the prospect a special offer for a limited time only (p. 110)

Specialty goods products about which consumers have knowledge and confidence, and for which they usually will not accept substitutes (p. 130)

Standing room only (SRO) closing method that suggests to the prospect that the product or service may not be available later (p. 110)

Substitution attempt to get a customer to buy something other than what was requested (p. 149)

Suggestive selling the face-to-face effort to motivate the customer to buy more now, and if done correctly, to buy more often (p. 146)

Summary of benefits closing method that involves restating benefits the customer will receive from the product or service (p. 110)

T
Telemarketing the structured use of the telephone to purchase or sell products or services, to obtain or give information to businesses and residences, or to solicit funds or support for charities, political parties, and other nonprofit organizations (p. 26)

GLOSSARY

Tickler file a file organized by dates (p. 117)

Track to follow the progress of an order through the fulfillment process (p. 39)

Trading up substituting a higher-priced line (p. 149)

Transaction selling the exchange of a product or service for the purchase price or the promise to pay the purchase price (p. 50)

Trial close tests to see how far along the prospect has come toward the buying decision (p. 109)

Turnover situation in which the salesperson turns the customer over to someone else in an effort to close the sale (p. 148)

U

Undecided customers prospects who do not know what to buy (p. 133)

W

Wholesaler sells products to retailers, other wholesalers, industrial firms, government agencies, or other businesses (p. 6)

INDEX

A
Acknowledgment
  e-mail, 39
  in retail selling, 139
Administrative tasks, 119
Advertising, media, 60
Agency relationship, 101–102
Amenities approach, 140
Antitrust laws, 104
Approach, in retail selling, 139–140
Attributes
  defined, 9
  See also Attributes for success
Attributes for success
  empathy, 10
  imagination, 11
  integrity, 10
  interpersonal skills, 12
  patience, 11–12
  persistence, 9–10
  product knowledge, 10
  self-motivation, 11
Automated sales presentations, 35

B
Barriers to listening, 16
Benefits
  defined, 48
  general benefit strategy, 55
  knowledge of, 54
  summary of, 110
Better Business Bureau, 61
Billing, fulfillment and, 38
Birthday offers, 147
Blind search, 59–60
Body language, 83, 100
Borders, Inc., 46
Bribes, 105
Business Math Connection
  breakeven point, 82
  invoices, 38
  mileage expenses, 118
  proving cash, 151
  retail prices, 57
  sales commission, 6

Buying decisions, retail, 135
Buying habits, 129
Buying motives, 49–50
Buying power, 73
Buying signals, 100

C
Calendar, 119
Canned presentation, 81
Careers in Selling
  Assistant Store Manager (MASM), 125
  Creative Memories Consultants, 70
  Customer Service Representative, 2
  In-Store Corporate Sales Representative (CSR), 46
  Investment Associate, 24
  Reservation Sales and Service Representative, 96
  Sales Associate, 2
  See also Sales career
Case histories, 56
Cash, in retail selling, 151–152
Cash drawer, proving, 151
Cashless payments, 74
Casual looker, 133
Catalog shopping, 130
Center-of-influence referral method, 61
Certified Life Underwriter (CLU), 55
Chamber of Commerce, 61
Charles Schwab & Co., Inc., 24
Chat rooms, customer, 40
Checks, in retail selling, 152
Clarification probe, 80
Clayton Act, 104–105
Closing
  approaches for, 98–101
  defined, 98
  laws and, 101–102
  methods of. See Closing methods
  objections and, 88
  overcoming fear of, 99

  pre-approach call, 76
  psychology of, 99
  in retail sales, 144
  timing for, 100
  unprofessional, 112
  unsuccessful, 99–100
  when answer is no, 111
Closing methods
  asking for action, 107–108
  assuming agreement, 107–108
  direct request, 109
  impending event, 109–110
  indirect request, 109
  narrowing the choice, 110
  special offer, 110
  standing room only (SRO), 110–111
  summary of benefits, 110
  using silence, 108
Code of Ethics, 105
Collusion, 105
Commission, sales, 6
Communicate feature
  Code of Ethics, 105
  e-mail acknowledgment, 39
  lead-qualifying script, 74
  open-ended questions, 52
  sales letter, 17
  suggestion selling, 147
Communication skills, 14–19
  e-mail, 18
  listening, 16–17
  sales letters, 17–18
  sales proposal, 18
  speaking, 14–16
Company knowledge, 57
Compatible merchandise, 147
Competition, knowledge about, 57
Complaints, 150
Conscientious prospecting style, 64
Consideration, 103
Consumer Product Safety Act of 1972, 104
Consumer spending, 6
Contact management software, 28

INDEX

Contracts, 102–103
  agency, 101–102
Convenience goods, 129
Creative Memories, 70
Credit approval, 38
Credit cards, 152
Credit standing, 73
Customer loyalty plans, 147
Customer profiles, 29
Customer relations, 132
Customers
  building trust with, 51
  buying decisions of retail, 135
  buying motives, 49–50
  dislikes among, 51
  follow up with. *See* Follow up
  handling multiple retail, 148
  maintaining contact with retail, 147
  moods of retail, 134
  retail, 132–135
  searching for, 59–62
  wants of, 48–50
Customer service, fulfillment and, 38
Customized presentation, 81

D

Database technology
  data management software, 28–29
  data mining, 29
  for prospecting, 61–62
Data management software, 28–29
Data mining
  defined, 29
  fulfillment and, 38
Debit cards, 152
Decided customers, 132, 141
Delta Airlines, 96
Direct Marketing Association, 26
Directories, prospecting with, 61
Direct request, 109
DISC Inventory, 63
Door-to-door sales, 60
Downloadable products, 33
Downtime, efficient use of, 118–119
Drive prospecting style, 63

E

E-commerce, 6
Economy, down turn in, 120
80-20 principle, 131
Elaboration probe, 80
E-mail
  marketing via, 62
  sales acknowledgment, 39
  sales promotion, 18
Emotional buying motives, 50
Emotional close, 112
Empathy, 10
Encouragement probe, 80
Enterprise-wide solutions, 28
Esteem needs, 49
Exchanges, 150–151
Exclusive dealerships, 105
Expertise, 55
Eye contact, 83

F

False labeling, 105
Fashionable merchandise, 147
Features
  defined, 48
  evidence of, 55–56
  knowledge of, 54
Federal Food, Drug, and Cosmetic Act, 104
Federal Trade Commission, 105
Financial sales, 7
Follow up, 114–117
  fulfillment, 37–39
  gifts and entertainment, 117
  letter, 115
  newsletter, 117
  online customer assistance, 40
  personal organizer and, 40
  personal touch for, 39–40
  service, 116
  technology for, 37–41
  tickler file, 117
  visits, 115–116
Food and Drug Administration (FDA), 104
Forecast, sales, 29
Foreign Commercial Service Programs, 89
Fraud, 105
Frequently asked questions (FAQs), 40
Fulfillment
  computer technology and, 39
  defined, 37
  nine steps to, 38
  salesperson's role in, 39

G

Gateway Computers, 143
General benefit strategy, 55
Give-up close, 112
Goal setting, 120
Greeting, 139
Group shopping, 148
Guarantee, 56

H

Handshake, 83
Heterogeneous shopping goods, 129
Home Depot, 125, 143
Home shopping, 130
Homogeneous shopping goods, 129

I

Imagination, 11
Impending event, 109–110
Impulse goods, 129
Inbound telemarketing, 27
Incentive programs, 62
Indirect request, 109
Industry, defined, 56
Industry knowledge, 56
Influencing ability prospecting style, 64
Integrity, 10
International Trade Administration, 89
Internet
  benefits of, 31
  as business tool, 32
  defined, 32
  downloadable products on, 33
  e-commerce, 6
  as networking tool, 62
  placing orders on, 33
  product information on, 33
  sales training via, 32–33

selling on, 33
shopping, 130
use of, 31–33
See also E-mail
Interpersonal skills, 12
Interview
   gaining, in retail selling, 139–140
   objections to gaining, 88
   techniques, for needs assessment, 79
Intranet, 32
Inventory control, 38
Invoices, 38

J
Just-looking customer, 133–134, 141

K
Key-point presentation, 81
Knowledge
   company, 57
   competitive, 57
   customer, 51
   industry, 56
   market, 56–57
   product or service, 54–56, 131

L
Lands' End, 2
Law(s)
   agency contracts and, 101–102
   antitrust, 104
   consumer protection, 104
   contracts, 102–103
   prohibited acts, 104–105
   telemarketing, 28
   torts, 102
   Uniform Commercial Code (UCC), 103
Lead qualification
   defined, 72
   reason for, 72–73
   script for, 74
   successful openings for calls, 75
   voice mail and, 73
Legally competent parties, 102

Letter, follow-up, 115
Listening skills, 16–17
   objections and, 90
   for relationship selling, 52
Lists, 61

M
Mailing list, retail, 147
Manufacturing salesperson, 6–7
Marketing
   database, 61–62
   e-mail, 62
Market knowledge, 56–57
Marston, William Moulton, 63
Maslow's Hierarchy of Needs
   buying motives and, 49–50
   objections and, 86–87
Media advertising, 60
Meeting
   pitch, 82–83
   unexpected, 109
Meeting skills, 15
Merchandise approach, 140
Mileage expenses, 118
Misrepresentation, 105
Monopolies, 104
Motivation, 49–50, 120

N
Narrowing the choice, 110
Needs
   Maslow's hierarchy of, 49–50
   recognized, 73
   satisfying, 50, 79
Needs assessment
   defined, 78
   developing and proposing solutions, 80
   establishing the need, 78–79
   interviewing techniques, 79
   probing for information, 79–80
Networking, 62
Newsletter, 117

O
Objections
   classifying, 87–89
   defined, 85

   disagreeing prospect and, 86–87
   handling, 85–87
   Maslow's needs hierarchy and, 86–87
   real vs. stall, 88
   recognizing, 86
   restating, 90
   in retail selling process, 138
   rules for handling, 89–90
   salesperson's attitude toward, 87
   salesperson's interruptions during, 90
   sales process phase and, 88
   validity of, 88
Offer and acceptance, 102–103
Online customer assistance, 40
Online orders, 33. *See also* Internet
Open-ended questions, 52
Order filling, 38
Order forms, 38
Order tracking, online customer, 40
Organizing
   administrative tasks, 119
   calendar, 119
   efficient use of downtime, 118–119
   planning sales calls, 118
Outbound telemarketing, 26–27

P
Patience, 11–12
Persistence, 9–10
Personal observation, prospecting through, 60
Personal organizer, 40, 119
Personal selling, 7, 48–50
   buying motives and, 49–50
   customer wants and, 48–50
   defined, 48
   need satisfaction and, 50
Physiological needs, 49
Pitch
   meeting, 82–83
   preparing for, 81
Pre-approach
   closing the call, 76

INDEX

defined, 72
first 30 seconds, 74–75
lead qualification, 72–73
in retail selling, 138
Presentation. *See* Pitch; Sales presentation
Presentation skills, 15–16
Presentation visuals, 34–35
Price discrimination, 105
Principal, 101–102
Probing, 79–80
Problem
   establishing, 141
   solving, 141–142
Problem resolution, 79
Product knowledge, 10, 54–56
   in retail selling, 131
   substitution and, 149
Product testing, 56
Project
   retail selling, 125
   sales career, 3
   preparing to sell, 47, 71, 97
   technology and selling, 25
Promotional merchandise, 147
Prospect
   assuming agreement of, 107–108
   expression of, closing and, 100
   disagreeing, 86–87
   meeting the, 82–83
Prospecting
   blind search, 59–60
   database marketing, 61–62
   defined, 59
   directories, 61
   door-to-door sales, 60
   e-mail marketing, 62
   lists, 61
   media advertising, 60
   networking, 62
   personal observation, 60
   referrals, 61
   in retail selling, 137–138
   selective search, 60–62
   styles of, 63–64
   telemarketing, 60
   telequalifying, 62
Proving cash, 151
Pure Food and Drug Act, 105

Q

Questions
   closing, 101
   open-ended, 52

R

Rational buying motives, 50
Reciprocity, 105
Recognition statements, 100–101
Referrals, 61, 75
Relationship selling, 51–52
   building trust and, 51
   customer knowledge and, 51
   filling customer needs and, 52
   listening and, 52
   open-ended questions for, 52
Repeat business, 39
Repeat customer, 5
Reports, fulfillment and, 38
Retail sales, 6
Retail selling, 125–157
   challenges, 130–131
   classifications of products, 128–129
   complaints, 150
   customers in, 132–135
   exchanges, 150
   group shopping, 148
   handling multiple customers, 148
   image of career in, 130
   paying for merchandise in, 151–152
   peak-valley nature of demand, 131
   requirements of, 131
   returned goods, 150
   sales process in, 137–143. *See also* Retail selling process
   sales records for, 150–152
   substitution, 149
   turnover, 148–149
   working conditions in, 131
Retail selling process
   after the sale, 146–147
   approach, 139–140
   closing, 144
   establishing and solving problem, 141–142
   gaining the interview, 139–140
   handling objections, 138
   pre-approach, 138
   prospecting, 137–138
Returned goods, 150–151
Robinson-Patman Act, 104
Routing calls, 118

S

Safety needs, 49
Sales automation, 28
Sales call
   average cost of, 27
   planning, 118
Sales career
   art of selling and, 4–5
   attributes for success in, 9–13
   communication skills for, 14–19
   occupational growth of, 5
   opportunities, 5–7
   project, 3
   retail, 130
   See also Careers in Selling
Sales commission, 6
Sales force, telemarketing working with, 27–28
Sales forecast, data mining and, 29
Sales kiosks, 130
Sales letters, 17–18
Salespeople
   attitude toward objections, 87
   earnings of, 109
   incentive programs for, 62
   indifference of, 130–131
   role in fulfillment, 39
Sales presentation
   automated, 35
   canned, 81
   customized, 81
   defined, 15
   key-point, 81
   technology for, 34–35
   visuals for, 34–35
Sales process
   closing, 98–113
   customer follow-up, 114–117
   handling objections, 85–91

INDEX

making pitch, 81–83
meeting needs, 78–80
objections and phases of, 88
pre-approach, 72–77
preparing to sell, 46–69
in retail selling, 137–143
Sales proposal, 18
Sales receipt, 150
Sales training, Internet, 32–33
Screeners, 73
Securities, commodities, and financial service representatives, 6–7
Security needs, 49
Selective search, 60–62
Self-actualization needs, 50
Self-checkout stations, 130
Self-motivation, 11
Self-service, 7
Selling
   art of, 4–5
   defined, 5
   knowledge for, 54–58
   psychology of, 48–53
Service, follow-up, 116
Service approach, 139–140
Service knowledge, 54–56
Sherman Act, 104–105
Shipping, fulfillment and, 38
Shopping goods, 129
Showdown close, 112
Silence
   probe, 79–80
   using, 108
Slow times, 120
Social needs, 49
Software
   contact management, 28
   data management, 28–29
Speaking skills, 14–16
   meetings, 15
   presentations, 15–16
   telephone conversations, 14–15
Specialty goods, 130
Special offer closing method, 110
Standard & Poor's rating, 73
Standing room only (SRO), 110–111

Stand merchandise, 147
Steadfast prospecting style, 64
Subliminal messages, in presentation visuals, 35
Substitution, 149
Suggestive selling, 146–147
Summary of benefits, 110

T

Team, telemarketing, 27
Team leader, 12
Teamwork, 12
Technology
   database, 28–29
   follow-up, 37–41
   Internet usage, 31–33
   presentation, 34–35
   telemarketing, 26–28
Tech Talk
   automated retail sales, 130
   cashless payments, 74
   e-commerce, 6
   rewarding salespeople, 62
   trade shows, 108
   wireless revolution, 29
Telemarketing, 26–28
   defined, 26
   inbound, 27
   legislative regulations for, 28
   outbound, 26–27
   prospecting through, 60
   sales force and, 27–28
   team, 27
   uses of, 27
Telemarketing Sales Rule, 28
Telephone conversations, 14–15
Telequalifying, 62
Testimonials, 56
Tickler file, 117
Tie-in sales, 105
To do list, 119
Topic-change probe, 80
Torts, 102
Track orders, 39
Trading up, 149
Transaction selling, 50
Trial close, 109
Turnover, 148–149

U

U.S. Department of Commerce, 89
Undecided customers, 133, 141
Uniform Commercial Code (UCC), 101–103
Unintentional negligence torts, 102

V

Visuals, presentation, 34–35
Voice mail, lead qualifying by, 73

W

Wheeler-Lea Act, 104
Wholesaler, 6–7
Workshop
   attributes for sales success, 10
   brainstorm products or services, 5
   calendar, 119
   center-of-influence referrals, 61
   classifying retail products, 129
   closing methods, 110
   company slogans, 17
   customer data, 29
   dishonest sales acts, 101
   lead-qualifying calls, 75
   Maslow's need hierarchy, 49
   presentation types, 81
   product testimonials, 56
   retail interview approaches, 139
   return policies, 152
   rules for objections, 89
   sales presentation visuals, 34
   web site experiences, 39
World View
   business card etiquette, 116
   business etiquette, 11
   business on the Net, 32
   getting off to global start, 89
   global sales success, 55
   needs of minority groups, 143

Y

Yellow Pages, 61

Z

Ziglar, Zig, 86, 109

PHOTO CREDITS

Cover art © EyeWire.
All photos © PhotoDisc, Inc.